HORSE BREEDS

65 Popular Horse, Pony, & Draft Horse Breeds

Daniel and Samantha Johnson

Voyageur
Press

First published in 2008 by Voyageur Press,
an imprint of MBI Publishing Company,
400 First Avenue North, Suite 300,
Minneapolis, MN 55401 USA

The information in this book is true and complete to the best
of our knowledge. All recommendations are made without any
guarantee on the part of the author or Publisher, who also disclaim
any liability incurred in connection with the use of this data or
specific details.

We recognize, further, that some words, model names, and
designations mentioned herein are the property of the trademark
holder. We use them for identification purposes only. This is not
an official publication.

Voyageur Press titles are also available at discounts in bulk quantity
for industrial or sales-promotional use. For details write to Special
Sales Manager at MBI Publishing Company, 400 First Avenue
North, Suite 300, Minneapolis, MN 55401 USA.

To find out more about our books,
join us online at www.voyageurpress.com.

ISBN-13: 978-0-7603-3265-8

Library of Congress Cataloging-in-Publication Data

Johnson, Samantha.
  Horse breeds : 65 popular horse, pony, & draft horse breeds / by
Samantha Johnson ; photos by Daniel Johnson.
      p. cm.
  Includes index.
  ISBN 978-0-7603-3265-8 (hb, plc)
1. Horse breeds. 2. Horse breeds Pictorial works. I. Johnson,
Daniel, 1984- II. Title.
SF291.J55 2008
636.1—dc22
                                    2008004098

Printed in China

About the Author and Photographer:
Samantha Johnson is the author of *How to Raise Horses* and
the *Field Guide to Rabbits*. She is a certified horse show judge
and has contributed articles to horse newsletters and magazines.
She lives in Phelps, Wisconsin.

Daniel Johnson, a widely published photographer, specializes in
equine photography. He also manages a family-owned horse farm,
where he oversees breeding, training, and showing. He lives in
Phelps, Wisconsin.

On the front cover:
The Welsh Cob (Section D) is an impressive breed with substance
and athleticism. All purebred Welsh Cobs in the United States
descend from stock that was initially imported from their native
country of Wales. Welsh Cobs excel in all performance areas, such
as dressage, eventing, and driving.

On the frontispiece:
Golden sunlight adds to the glow of this Haflinger's already golden
head. Haflingers have pretty, attractive pony heads with kind, large
eyes set rather forward on the face. This, in addition to the breed's
already good general conformation, makes them the choice of
many pony enthusiasts.

On the title pages:
The blue sky beautifully accentuates the colors of these lovely horses.
The palomino American Quarter Horse on the left grazes next to a
black-and-white Pinto that exhibits the overo color pattern.

On the back cover:
Two horses enjoy a peaceful summer evening in a meadow. The
differences in size and build are clearly llustrated between these
two breeds: a Tennessee Walking Horse and a Pinto horse.

Editor: Amy Glaser

Designer: Cindy Samargia Laun

CONTENTS

DEDICATION

To Patricia Behling for coming along on many of the summer photo shoots and keeping us company on the long drives, for always being an encouraging voice, and for always seeing the cup as half full. We love you!

ACKNOWLEDGMENTS

It would take a long list and a great deal of space to give thanks to all those who make a book like this possible, but to scratch the surface we must begin with our editor, Amy Glaser, for her continued support and encouragement throughout this book's development. Thanks Amy! Thanks to our wonderful family who continues to encourage us and give us the incredible support required to finish a project of this magnitude.

A big thanks must go out to all those who helped us locate horse models and to the owners who so graciously opened their barns and farms to Dan so he could photograph their animals. We appreciate your kindness and generosity and we hope that you enjoy seeing your horses and ponies pictured in this book. Specific thanks as always to Jayme Nelson and the Pine Ridge Equestrian Center. Also thanks to Jim, Reita, and Tasha Gelander for the fun visit, and to Miracle Welsh Ponies and Cobs for allowing us unlimited access to their beautiful ponies.

Thanks to J. Keeler Johnson for helping out and supplying some of his fantastic horse images; the book wouldn't have been complete without them. Of course, we couldn't have completed this project without the help of Dan's beloved "Baby" and her powerful lens.

Also thanks to our longtime pals Whitney and Violet. Thanks for all the laughs!

INTRODUCTION

A large herd of horses makes its
way down a well-beaten path from
the barn to the pasture and displays
a wide variety of sizes, types, coat
colors, and coat patterns.

When you think of the different breeds of horses, which ones come to mind? Thoroughbreds, perhaps? Arabians? Quarter Horses? Perhaps you think of adorable Miniature Horses—or are they colorful Pinto horses? How about those impressive black horses, the Friesians? Those are all excellent choices, yet they barely scratch the surface of the vast myriad of horse and pony breeds. Within this book, we will present many of the world's most cherished and popular

These two equines share a pasture, but their backgrounds are very different. The Chincoteague Pony on the left hails from a small island off the coast of Virginia, while the substantial Shire draft horse on the right is an English breed.

horse breeds, along with a few of the more unusual ones, in an entertaining, exciting photo-driven format. This book, with its vivid imagery and detailed text, will usher you into the beautiful world of equines by exploring more than 65 breeds of horses and ponies. You'll feel the wind rush past you as a galloping Thoroughbred thunders by. You'll stand in awe at the legendary beauty of the ancient Arabian. You'll discover the delights of the British native ponies and admire the amazing power and gentle dispositions of the heavy draft breeds.

The equine world encompasses many different types of horses used for a variety of different purposes—from trail riding to fox hunting. From the tiniest backyard leadline pony to a 17-hand Warmblood competing at the Olympics, there is a breed to suit everyone's needs or desires. For that reason we have divided this book into five manageable sections. We'll begin our journey with a study of the world's pony breeds; the cute, small, yet athletic and versatile equines. From there we will jump into the light horse breeds and discover more about many of the world's most popular breeds, as well as a few breeds that are not so well known. Then it's on to examine horses of a different color or many different colors! The colored horse chapter covers horses with specific or unique coat patterns, from Appaloosas to American Paint Horses, and even some lesser-defined breeds/colors, such as the Palomino. From there we will

This attractive Warmblood epitomizes the look and presence sought after by enthusiasts. His broad forehead, small ears, and lovely expression make him a showstopper in the show ring. Presence is often described as a "look at me" attitude, which this gelding certainly possesses.

discover the horse world's gentle giants in the heavy horse chapter. Finally, we'll close with a chapter devoted to our favorite "long ears," which is a look at the various types of donkeys and mules. May you experience the joy that comes from discovering a breed of horse or pony that completely fulfills your equine dreams, and may you fully enjoy the process of dreaming about horses and ponies!

A grey Welsh-Thoroughbred mare performs a hunter course at an open hunter/jumper show. The Welsh Pony and Cob Society of America maintains a half-Welsh registry for animals with a purebred, registered Welsh parent. This pony's sire was a registered Section B Welsh Pony and her dam was a Thoroughbred.

PONIES

The striking, chiseled, dished face of the Welara is one of the ultimate goals of the breeder who aims to combine the beauty of the Arabian with the Welsh Pony. The cross has certainly paid off in this case.

With their large eyes, tiny ears, substantial bodies, and hardy constitutions, ponies are undeniably endearing. While it's commonly understood that ponies are small equines standing less than 14.2 hands, it's also important to understand that pony breeds exhibit different characteristics than horse breeds. Ponies typically have a more compact build than horses, with small heads that often exhibit a dished (concave) profile rather than a Roman nose (convex) profile. In addition, the legs of a pony are shorter than a horse's in terms of leg-to-body ratio. Ponies are notably hardy, healthy, and often known as "easy-keepers" due to their ability to maintain good weight and body condition on small amounts of food. Generally, pony breeds have very long life expectancies (35 to 40 years) and delightfully charming personalities, in addition to being very intelligent.

While many equine owners prefer horses, the mantra of pony enthusiasts worldwide is that bigger is not always better. Pony fans are eager to dispel the myth that ponies are only for children. While there is no denying that ponies are an ideal choice for children, it's also true that many pony breeds are large enough and capable enough to carry adults. Many adult riders are not interested in riding or caring for an equine that is 16 hands or taller and find great joy and fun with ponies. Additionally, ponies are popular choices as driving animals for adults.

A Shetland Pony stands near a full-sized horse. Despite the great difference in size, the Shetland Pony fits well into the herd's dynamics and is able to keep its place in the pecking order.

Many pony breeds originated in the United Kingdom, and the majority of these U.K. breeds are known as British native ponies. There is a growing interest in the United States for British native pony breeds, with classes for Mountain and Moorland Ponies appearing at many horse shows nationwide.

Native to Ireland, the Connemara Pony is popular as a performance pony because of its talent and athleticism as well as its very useful size (more than 13 hands). The native Connemara breed goes back to before the thirteenth century and has been influenced by an infusion of Welsh Cob, Thoroughbred, and Arabian blood, thus increasing the overall quality of the original native ponies. Today, the Connemara is one of the most popular native pony breeds.

Another native Irish pony breed is the Kerry Bog. The name comes from the ponies' original home along the bogs of Ireland, where they have survived for centuries in their natural state. Selective breeding of Kerry Bog Ponies began in the 1990s and interest is steadily increasing, although there are only a few Kerry Bog Ponies in the United States. Kerry Bog Ponies are small, measure under 12 hands, and have a lightness of step that is the result of the breed's development on the bogs of Ireland.

Due in part to the influence from and similarities to the Appaloosa, the Pony of the Americas (POA) has gained a reputation of being a fine show pony for Western disciplines. While the head and face of the breed typically shows distinct pony character, the POA is a definite stock-type pony.

Two close cousins in the world of British native ponies are the Dales and Fell Ponies. Originally called Pennine Ponies, they were subsequently divided into two separate breeds. Both breeds are frequently found in black, but other colors are also seen. The Dales Pony, measuring as large as 14.2 hands, is somewhat larger than the Fell.

A bay Welsh Cob (Section D) stallion enjoys running loose in the pasture after being turned out for the morning. The largest of the four Welsh sections, the Welsh Cob usually stands in the range of 14.2 hands, although there is no upper height limit. Some breeders call the smaller, more compact Welsh Cobs the Cardiganshire-type, and the taller, leggier Welsh Cobs are referred to as the Breconshire-type.

The Fell is not usually over 14 hands. Both of these native breeds have been influenced by the Friesian, although the Fell bears the greater resemblance to that breed.

One of the smallest of the British native ponies, the Dartmoor stands less than 12 hands and originally roamed the moorlands in Devon, England. The Dartmoor has been influenced by several other breeds, including the Welsh Mountain Pony, Arabian, Shetland Pony, and Fell Pony. As is the case with other native breeds, Dartmoors are typically found in dark colors, such as brown or bay. One notable characteristic of the Dartmoor is that it trots with a significant lack of knee action unlike other pony breeds, such as the Hackney or the Welsh Mountain Pony that often trot with considerable knee action.

While the Dartmoor Pony was somewhat altered by the infusion of other breeds, the Exmoor Pony, which made its home in the hills of England, is regarded as one of the purest of the British native pony breeds. The Exmoor is slightly larger than the Dartmoor and is particularly noted for its hardy character and uniform brown color. The Exmoor features a lighter-colored muzzle, which

Children and ponies seem to go together. With proper training and a little love, this pony will make a child's perfect companion for years to come. The smaller size and kind temperaments of ponies allow children to perform many of the basic horse care tasks by themselves, which might be too difficult for them to do with a larger horse. Ponies are also easier for children to control while riding because the child is properly proportioned to the pony in size, such as this little girl and her Welsh Mountain Pony mare.

is known as "mealy mouthed." Exmoors are well suited to a rugged lifestyle on the moors and exhibit a unique two-layered coat that is adept at repelling water.

Written documentation of the history of the New Forest Pony exists dating back to the tenth century. This attractive breed has achieved popularity in both the U.K. and the U.S. The breed has been influenced by many other native pony breeds, as well as Thoroughbred and Arabian horses. With the improved quality that resulted from the 1891 formation of the Society for Improvement of the New Forest Ponies, the New Forest Ponies of today are athletic and talented individuals that are slightly taller than some of the other native breeds and also a bit more refined.

Turning away from England for a moment, let's take a look at a native pony breed that hails from Scottish shores. Descended from the ancient native ponies of Scotland, the Highland Pony has been influenced by large draft breeds, such as the Percheron and Clydesdale. Because of this, the Highland Pony of today is a substantial, solid individual. Some Highland Ponies still exhibit primitive coloring, complete with dorsal stripes and leg barring. Historically, Highland Ponies were used by Scottish crofters and farmers in their daily work, and the breed is noted for its strength, stamina, and hardiness.

Here is an attractive chestnut Chincoteague Pony. The breed comes in a very wide range of colors with both solid and pinto coat patterns. The Chincoteague is a popular choice with children who dream of attending the annual pony penning event and adopting a pony.

Tiny in size but vast in strength, the original Shetland Pony endured centuries of rugged existence on the Shetland Islands. Shetland Ponies were commonly used in coal mines during the mid-1800s and were highly valued for their strength and stamina. They have long been revered as wonderful children's ponies with their diminutive size making them well-suited for the task. The original U.K. Shetlands are substantially different from the Modern American Shetland, which has taken on a great deal of refinement due to crossbreeding.

Now to the lovely Welsh breeds. There are four different varieties in this category, and it is best to look at each one individually. In their native Wales, each variation is considered to be its own breed, while in the U.S., they are considered to be one breed with four distinct sections.

The Welsh Mountain Pony (Section A) is a hardy, attractive pony that is widely cited as being the most beautiful pony breed in the world. The Section A is considered to be the purest of the four Welsh breeds and capable of improving any of the other three. The smallest of the four Welsh sections, Welsh Mountain Ponies stand less than 12.2 hands in the U.S., while the upper height limit in the U.K. is only 12 hands. The ponies are a favored choice as first ridden mounts for children but are also very popular as driving animals.

American Quarter Ponies can be fun for everyone and not just the kids! Here we catch a glimpse at some of the action during an obstacle driving course at an open driving show. Even though American Quarter Ponies are noted for their stock-type or Western appearance, they are versatile enough to be used for any number of equine activities.

Next in line is the Welsh Pony (Section B), which is a taller, more refined version of the Section A. It stands as tall as 14.2 hands in the U.S. and up to 13.2 hands in the U.K. Welsh Ponies are outstanding performance ponies and are seen all over the world competing in classes under saddle and over fences. They retain the distinct Welsh characteristics of beauty and quality and have been bred specifically as children's ponies since the mid-twentieth century.

A pretty, young Welara foal checks out the new sights, sounds, and surroundings of her first trip to the show grounds. Many owners and breeders find it wise to expose their foals to new sights and experiences early on. It is this early training that can make for a more sensible and tranquil animal later on.

The Welsh Pony of Cob Type (Section C) is the rarest of the four Welsh breeds, but it is rapidly gaining popularity in both the U.K. and the U.S. The height limit in both countries is 13.2 hands, but the Section C differs greatly from the Section B in terms of breed type, despite their similarity in size. While the Section B is typically an elegant pony with grace and refinement, the Section C is ideally a smaller, more compact version of a Welsh Cob. Section Cs are noted for their immense substance, strength, power, and stamina, and yet they still possess inherent Welsh type (such as large, expressive eyes and short, flat cannon bones). Section Cs are becoming very popular as driving ponies, particularly in combined driving events.

Finally, there is the Welsh Cob (Section D). This is a massive, powerful animal that stands over 13.2 hands with no upper height limit. The Welsh Cob has substantial bone structure, stamina, strength, and beauty. They are particularly noted for their breathtaking action at the trot and for their natural athleticism. Section Ds are gaining extensive exposure as dressage mounts because their quality of movement and temperament make them an ideal choice for this discipline. All sections of Welsh are great jumpers, which makes Welsh Cobs a great choice for the sport of eventing.

A refined and elegant British Riding Pony is trotting and showing off some of the lovely movement that the breed is noted for. Such ponies are often found competing in English-type classes at shows, both in-hand and under saddle.

Some of the most beautiful ridden ponies in the world are British Riding Ponies. Their refinement, elegance, and overall beauty make them a sight to behold. British Riding Ponies are produced through selective crossing of native ponies (such as Welsh or Connemara) with horse breeds (such as Thoroughbred or Arabian). The resulting British Riding Ponies, with their increased size and overall athletic ability, make them ideal candidates for children's ponies.

The beautiful dappled grey coloring of this gelding is commonly found in the Connemara breed. Also typical of the breed is a fine, attractive head and neck. Although Connemaras can be larger than 14.2 hands, the Connemara is still called a pony.

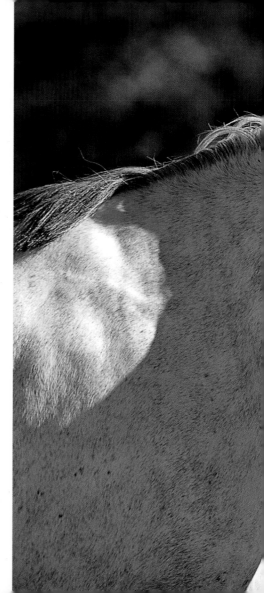

The most distinguishing characteristic of the Hackney Pony is its animated, high-stepping trot. Developed during the latter part of the nineteenth century, the Hackney Pony is a blend of Hackney horse crossed with Fell and Welsh Ponies. The extravagant action found in the Hackney Pony is credited to the Fell Pony influence. Hackney Ponies are extremely popular as harness ponies, particularly in the United States. Hackneys are typically a dark color, such as bay or black, and usually stand between 12 and 14 hands tall.

Although it may begin to seem as if all pony breeds originated in the United Kingdom, there are numerous pony breeds that have been developed in other countries. At this point, we will turn our attention to pony breeds that have developed elsewhere in the world.

While not considered a typical pony in type and characteristics (they actually resemble a small horse), the Caspian is recognized in this chapter due to its size: 10 to 12 hands, on average. It is generally accepted that the Caspian is among the oldest breeds of horses and possibly predates the Arabian. A fascinating history precedes the Caspian. The breed was assumed extinct until the 1960s when, amazingly, a woman named Louise Firouiz discovered a few remaining ponies in Iran. Due to her dedicated efforts to preserve the ancient breed, Caspians are now found in several countries and are being perpetuated through many breeding programs to ensure the breed's continued survival.

Because Shetland Ponies developed in the harsh conditions of the Shetland Islands, they are hardy, resourceful, and capable of thriving in almost any climate.

Very different in type than the Caspian is the Haflinger, a substantial breed that originated in Austria. The Arabian is the foundation breed for the Haflinger, which is somewhat surprising considering the sturdy mountain-type characteristics found in the Haflinger breed. Haflingers are noted for their longevity, and some live to the advanced age of 40. Another established characteristic of the Haflinger is its distinctive coloring—a rich, deep chestnut accompanied by a white mane and tail.

A herd of Miniature Horses is enjoying a day at pasture. Horse herds are typically led by a boss or alpha mare who has achieved dominance over the others. This is not necessarily determined by size or age, but is sorted out by body language and through the herd's personal dynamics.

Another breed that is highly recognized for its coloring is the Norwegian Fjord. Always a shade of dun, the Norwegian Fjord hails from Norway and has since gained popularity with enthusiasts as a harness horse. In appearance, the Norwegian Fjord is reminiscent of the ancient Przewalskis horse. The Fjord was used by the Vikings in Scandinavia centuries ago. The breed has also been widely used as a farm horse. The Fjord's popularity has spread across the world, and today they are commonly used as light draft harness horses.

This Norwegian Fjord stallion exhibits the grey dun coloring, which is one of the less common colors found in Norwegian Fjords. Other shades of dun include the brown dun (the most frequently seen shade), red dun, white dun, and the rare yellow dun.

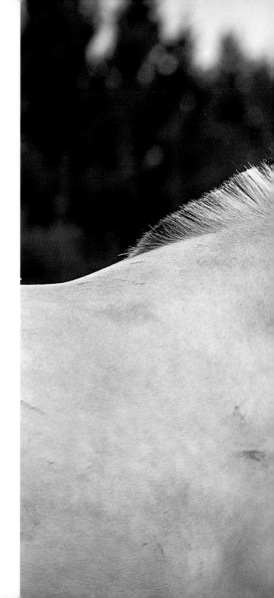

Although relatively new to North American shores, the German Riding Pony is quickly gaining interest among pony enthusiasts who are seeking a sport-type pony, as opposed to the more traditional hunter pony. The German Riding Pony, or *Deutsche Reitpony*, as it is known in Germany, is well suited to dressage due to its movement and build. German Riding Ponies have similar ancestry to British Riding Ponies but have been selected with emphasis on different characteristics. The French have also developed a riding pony variety of their own, known as the French Riding Pony, or the *Poney Francais de Selle*, although interest in the French Riding Pony has not matched that of the German Riding Pony in the United States.

The United States is responsible for creating several pony breeds. Perhaps the most distinctive, in looks and in name, is the Pony of the Americas, or POA as it is commonly called. The POA is one of a handful of breeds that can trace its foundation back to a single stallion, Black Hand 1, a Shetland Pony/Appaloosa/Arabian cross-foaled in Iowa in 1954. Breeders were immediately intrigued by the unusual colt, who combined the characteristics of the Shetland Pony and the Arabian, with the bonus of the Appaloosa coloring. Subsequently, other breeds were used to further develop the POA, including Quarter Horses, Welsh Ponies, Morgans, and Thoroughbreds. While the POA is often recognized

Autumn colors present the perfect backdrop to showcase this lovely Welsh-Thoroughbred mare. The idea behind creating this cross was to combine the stamina, athleticism, and talent of the Thoroughbred with the smaller size, beauty, and lovely head of the Welsh Pony. The cross seems to have worked well here.

for its natural abilities as a stock-type pony excelling in Western disciplines, POA enthusiasts have discovered the POA's versatility and athleticism and use them in other disciplines. They are typically shown by children, although many adults also enjoy the POA.

Although the United States is credited as being the country of origin of the Welara Pony, the truth is that the breed was initially developed through the vision of Lady Judith Wentworth in the U.K. The Welara, as the name implies, was created by crossing Welsh Ponies with Arabian horses, which Lady Wentworth began doing in the first half of the twentieth century. Her goal was to combine the characteristics of her two favorite breeds into one package with the aim of increasing the size of the Welsh Pony while accentuating the beauty, endurance, and athleticism prized in Arabian horses. One of the influential early stallions was Wentworth's own Arabian stallion, Skowronek. Even though the Welsh/Arabian ponies were bred for several decades by enthusiasts throughout the world, a registry was not set up until January 15, 1981, when the American Welara Pony Registry was formed. The ideal size for a Welara ranges between 46 and 60 inches, although individuals outside of these parameters are not excluded from registration.

The American Quarter Pony does not have an extremely strict breed standard, as its registry was initially established to record, register, and open up showing opportunities to small horses and ponies of unknown background. Generally, the breed should feature a Western or stock-type build and stand under 14.2 hands. Very small ponies are discouraged from registration.

Probably no other pony breed has enjoyed greater publicity and promotion than the Chincoteague Pony, thanks to Marguerite Henry's beloved 1947 classic *Misty of Chincoteague,* and the subsequent film *Misty,* which was released in 1961. Chincoteague Ponies are found on the islands of Assateague and Chincoteague, near Virginia, where they still roam wild today. According to legend, the wild Chincoteague

Weigel

A Welsh Cob (Section D) mare grazes peacefully in the late afternoon sunlight. Many of the first Welsh Ponies and Cobs registered in the Welsh Pony and Cob Society (U.K.) at the beginning of the twentieth century were named Bess or Lady Bess after Queen Elizabeth, who overturned King Henry XIII's attempts to destroy all ponies.

Ponies descend from horses that were shipwrecked hundreds of years ago; however, no evidence has been found to substantiate this claim. Each year, a pony penning event takes place where the ponies swim across to Chincoteague Island from Assateague and an auction is held to allow buyers to purchase young Chincoteague Ponies. The remaining ponies are then taken back to Assateague. Over several centuries of being left in their natural state, the Chincoteague

A Miniature Horse stallion runs through his pasture for an afternoon gallop. Even though it is much smaller than a traditional horse, the ideal Miniature will still maintain the leg-to-body ratio of a horse, rather than a pony, whose legs are somewhat shorter in proportion.

breed developed certain conformational inadequacies, which included an overall coarseness. Measures have been taken to improve the overall quality of the ponies by introducing new blood (including Shetland, Arabian, Welsh, and Mustang) into the wild herds.

We have already discussed the delightful Shetland Pony, which is a perennial favorite in the U.K. and U.S. alike. However, breeders in the United States have also developed a revised version of the Shetland Pony, which is known as the Modern American Shetland, and is very different in type than the classic Shetland. This is due to crossbreeding that has occurred in the United States to bring infusions of outside blood (notably Hackney, but also Arabian, Thoroughbred, and Welsh) into the Shetlands, which has resulted in a more refined pony with longer legs and an exaggerated trot. These characteristics are prized by harness pony enthusiasts, and many of the Modern American Shetlands are utilized for this purpose.

One of the newest names in American ponies is the American Sport Pony. The American Sport Pony Registry (ASPR) opened in 1997 as a subdivision of the American Warmblood Registry. The American Sport Pony is not a breed in the traditional meaning of the word. It is considered to be more of a type than a breed. The paramount emphasis of the ASPR is the promotion of a quality

POAs make wonderful children's ponies and are very popular for this purpose, and it is easy to see why. What child wouldn't fall in love with this breed's easy, gentle disposition; natural athletic abilities; and attractive coloring? The POA makes a perfect all-around family animal.

sport-type pony, which is ideally a miniature version of the traditional sport horse. There are other breed registries that recognize sport ponies, including the International Sport Horse Registry (ISR) and the Rheinland Pfalz-Saar International (RPSI), however each organization's registration requirements are a bit different with varying emphasis on certain characteristics.

Another American pony creation is the American Quarter Pony, which is also considered a type rather than a breed. The American Quarter Pony Registry was formed in the 1960s in an effort to provide grade ponies with the opportunity to compete in horse show classes restricted to registered animals. The American Quarter Pony can be any breed or mixture of breeds, although there are some restrictions on color, size, and type. No gaited ponies are eligible for registration, nor are ponies that do not fall between the size parameters of 46 to 57 inches. The American Quarter Pony exhibits Western stock type and is a useful, all-around pony that averages about 13.2 hands.

Similar in type to the American Quarter Pony, yet in a more colorful variety, is the American Paint Pony. The American Paint Pony Registry was established in 1972, and while the registry allows ponies of many different breeds, many are

The Welsh Pony of Cob Type (Section C) is a more compact and scaled-down version of its larger Section D cousin. While physical appearances between the two are similar, the Section C usually has a more pony-like head and can reach an upper height limit of only 13.2 hands, which is well within pony size. Don't be fooled; the Section C is still a powerful animal and well loved by a small but growing nucleus of breeders and owners.

of American Quarter Horse or American Paint Horse backgrounds. The registry does not permit gaited ponies or ponies with Appaloosa characteristics, and ponies must meet the criteria for necessary white markings. The ideal size of the American Paint Pony is 12 to 14.2 hands, although smaller ponies may be registered in the pee wee division.

Golden sunlight streams through the mane of this young Welsh Mountain Pony (Section A) filly. Palominos have been a favorite of horse lovers for generations, and why not? With a pleasing yellow-gold tint combined with the already charming looks and temperament of this filly, she will certainly bring happiness and pleasure to some child or adult for years to come.

Finally we have the Miniature Horse, which is exactly what its name indicates. It is a miniature horse rather than a pony, although some might assume that they are ponies due to their diminutive size. There are two associations that provide registrations for miniature horses: the American Miniature Horse Association, which registers horses that stand 34 inches and under; and the American Miniature Horse Registry, which divides its registrations into two classifications. Division A is for horses 34 inches and under, and Division B is for horses that stand over 34 inches and less than 38 inches. Although they are generally too small to be ridden except by very small children, Miniature Horses are popular as driving horses and as pets and are also economical to keep.

A black-and-white pinto Shetland Pony trots through the green grass of his field and exhibits the typical movement still found in U.K Shetlands. This movement has been slightly altered due to crossbreeding in the United States.

A contented Haflinger rests in a field at the end of the day. The Haflinger is a substantial, surefooted, and sound breed with a muscular build. All purebred Haflingers descend from seven stallion lines, each represented by a different letter or combination of letters.

Opposite: Chincoteague Ponies are technically considered horses because their characteristics are more horse-like, including the fact that their leg-to-body ratio matches that of a horse and not a pony. However, with the breed height average at only 12 hands, Chincoteagues are affectionately called ponies. It has been suggested that this small stature is a result of the horses' adequate but simple island diet.

Two rather unusual grey dun Norwegian Fjords play with each other in a field. The black stripe down the middle of a Norwegian Fjord's mane is known as a *midtstol*, while the black stripe in the tail is known as a *halefjaer*.

A young rider and her British Riding
Pony stand outside the show ring after
performing in an English pleasure class.
The beauty and elegance of the British
Riding Pony, along with its natural
athleticism and flair, make it a winning
combination as a children's show mount
both in flat classes and over fences.

Here stands a Division B Miniature Horse posing for a conformation photograph. The American Miniature Horse Registry has two divisions based only on height, not type: Division A horses may measure up to 34 inches tall, and Division B horses can be as tall as 38 inches.

Opposite: A classic example of a Welsh Mountain Pony (Section A) mare with a beautiful head and movement. Grey is a common color in this breed due to the widespread influence of the breed's grey foundation stallions: Dyoll Starlight, Coed Coch Glyndwr, and Clan Pip.

The Welsh Cob (Section D) brings literal meaning to the word horsepower! A breed well known and respected for its endurance and stamina for trotting over long distances, the Welsh Cob also makes a fine riding animal. Owners enjoy its easy-going and docile temperaments, while spectators are bound to be attracted to the breed's fabulous movement.

Carriage driving classes are often popular events at shows, and not only for the drivers. Spectators enjoy watching these beautiful animals trot around the ring pulling attractive carriages. Classes such as this are judged on the turnout and appointments and the pony's way of going and manners. In a reinsmanship class, the skill of the driver is also tested.

Hardiness is a well-known and well-documented aspect of the Welsh Mountain Pony (Section A). After years of surviving in the harsh and difficult environment of its native habitat on the hills of Wales, the Welsh Mountain Pony can handle and enjoy itself even in cold and snowy conditions. This mare glides effortlessly through the deep snow and stays warm with an incredibly thick winter coat commonly seen in the pony breeds.

A newborn Welsh Mountain Pony foal snuggles peacefully into the deep soft straw of its stall. Within a short number of hours, the foal will be standing, nursing, playing, and attempting to trot about. Of course, it will spend a lot of time sleeping and laying down as well.

A Welsh-Thoroughbred cross takes a fence during a hunter class at a local horse show. The ideal hunter pony will be graceful, athletic, and refined, all of which are attributes that this cross displays. The crossing of a Welsh Pony and a Thoroughbred has become quite popular in an effort to combine the excellent characteristics of both breeds into one athletic, willing, and beautiful animal. They are popular as show animals in English riding events of all types.

Opposite: This black Fell Pony poses for a portrait just before entering his class at a show for Mountain and Moorland pony breeds. The attractive Fell Pony, a breed similar to the Dales Pony, is used often as a riding animal, although its abilities in harness are just as impressive.

The Connemara is a versatile, athletic pony well-suited to a wide range of disciplines from driving to dressage and jumping to an all-around children's mount. Here a Connemara gelding shows off his moves for the camera by displaying a controlled and well-collected canter.

The ideal Miniature Horse will be as small as possible while maintaining the characteristics of a full-sized horse. One of the smallest Miniature Horses ever recorded was named Little Pumpkin who stood a petite 14 inches tall.

Opposite: A young girl holds the lead of her Miniature Horse as the golden light of sunset falls over the grass. The small size of the Miniature Horse makes them an ideal size for children.

Two Welsh Mountain Pony foals play and race each other through the sunset light. The black roan colt and the palomino filly illustrate the wide variety of colors that are found in the Welsh Mountain Pony.

A young Norwegian Fjord foal pauses briefly before returning to the rest of the herd in the distance. When he is finished growing, this foal will probably stand around 14 hands, the average height for the breed.

Opposite: "The most beautiful pony breed in the world" is how the Welsh Mountain Pony (Section A) is often described and many agree. With their attractive, Arabian-like dished heads and their beautiful type and movement, the popularity of the Welsh Mountain Pony remains strong worldwide.

Something has grabbed the attention
of this Welsh Cob (Section D) mare.
Horses are naturally curious and
cautious animals who will carefully
examine and assess a new or
potentially frightening situation.
The Welsh breeds are known for
their large and expressive eyes.

In addition to being a perfect children's mount, the Welsh Mountain Pony (Section A) makes a snazzy driving pony. When fully hitched in a driving harness such as this, the Section A is a popular and very capable force in the driving ring.

Opposite: Shetland Ponies are known for their longevity, with some living into their 30s. This elderly mare is in her late 20s but still remains useful and continues to give enjoyment to her owners. Naturally, a pony will grow less spirited and become more of a "been there, done that" type as it enters its later years.

A cute and strikingly handsome black-and-white American Paint Pony dashes across his pasture. Although small, this pony has come to excel at the sport of dressage thanks to careful training by its owners.

Three Norwegian Fjords graze together. These Norwegian Fjords have had their manes trimmed in the traditional manner to show off the breed's unique and attractive mane coloring.

Two Welsh Mountain Ponies (Section A) prepare to enter a Multiple Draft Driving class. The team must be well trained and able to work well together since an error on one side of the team will affect the other. Some equines become quite emotionally attached to their driving partners after spending so much time working together.

Left: This Shetland Pony gelding will certainly be the perfect companion for this little girl. While strong and agile enough to perform any task she may ask of him later on, the pony is small enough and has the proper temperament to keep her experiences safe and fun.

Right: A polo pony is not considered a breed but is classified by a particular set of characteristics that lend themselves to being useful for the game. The horses are usually small so they are quicker to turn, brake, and accelerate.

The mane and tail of a spirited grey Welara mare catch the morning sunlight as she prances about. Welaras are a beautiful combination of the parent breeds and exhibit the look and presence that the Arabian and Welsh Pony are noted for, as well as maintaining a kind disposition.

An attractive liver chestnut America Quarter Pony mare is at liberty. The American Quarter Pony Association puts a great emphasis on the fact that the American Quarter Pony should be a family animal, and the registry's point system for shows reflects this philosophy.

Opposite: Haflingers excel in many venues, especially driving. Their gentle nature and pleasant attitudes make them a first choice of many horse owners wanting a smaller animal to show or enjoy. It addition to driving, Haflingers make calm and sound children's ponies.

A quiet moment at the end of the day. A young girl and her Welsh-Thoroughbred pony pause together for a moment before heading back to the stable.

Opposite: A wide smile crosses the face of this young rider who has just finished up a successful round in the hunter ring. Many children enjoy the quiet and obedient attitudes of ponies like the American Paint Pony.

This stallion gazes out intently, carefully watching something that has captured his attention. The German Riding Pony has been described as a small Warmblood and is noted for its pony quality and attractive face and size while maintaining the build and look of a Warmblood. The breed is starting to become a popular sport pony in the United States.

This American Paint Pony mare displays a lovely coat pattern in addition to an overall stock-type build, which is a winning combination to many enthusiasts. Unlike the Pony of the Americas, the American Paint Pony should not display any Appaloosa coat patterns.

Opposite: The attractive face of the Highland Pony is indicative of the Arabian blood in the breed's background. Today the Highland Pony's good-natured temperament and sturdiness make it a fine family animal.

A Miniature Horse mare watches carefully as her baby leaps and jumps about the pasture. Throughout history, the Miniature Horse has been used for a variety of tasks, from a hardworking life in the mines to a relaxing life as a beloved pet and companion.

Are these two different breeds? Actually it is a visual gauge of the wide range of sizes possible within the Welsh sections. Here a young palomino Welsh Mountain Pony (Section A) filly grazes next to her best friend, a large and robust bay Welsh Cob (Section D) mare.

A flashy Pony of the Americas mare with a leopard spot coat pattern gallops across an arena. This breed brings the popular and familiar Appaloosa coat patterns to a new height, although a slightly smaller one! The spots of a POA must be large enough to be visible at distances of at least 40 feet. The POA usually stands between 12.2 and 13.2 hands.

Opposite: A Haflinger gelding walks up along the fence line of his pasture. Like almost all Haflingers, this one shows the common chestnut coloring often associated with the breed. The golden coat with the flaxen mane and tail make the Haflinger one of the most attractive pony breeds.

A two-week-old chestnut Welsh Mountain Pony foal experiments with tasting some grass. She already displays the characteristics for which the breed is famous: beautiful face with large eyes, lengthy neck, and strong hindquarters.

Dales Ponies have proven their value as farm animals for years by working the land, pulling farm equipment, and working in coal mines. This Dales Pony eyes the photographer while the farm's large red barn stands guard in the background.

Foals require a natural, healthy, and
happy environment to grow up in,
with plenty of room to run and play.
Foals usually spend a great deal of
time swapping between play and rest.
This two-week-old Welsh Mountain
Pony filly is happily enjoying a
peaceful morning.

Polo, which is basically hockey on horseback, is an exciting and fast-paced game that has been in existence for centuries. Players on two separate teams compete to strike a ball into the opponent's goal with mallets, all while galloping, twisting, turning, and maneuvering on horseback. The action is swift and quick and lends itself to being a great spectator sport.

Opposite: A Welsh Pony of Cob Type (Section C) stallion strikes a brief pose for the camera. With its muscular body and compact, powerful build, the Section C is well-known for its ability as a driving animal and is prized for its brilliant movement and stamina. One of the most famous Section Cs of modern times is Cefnoakpark Bouncer, who won an FEI Driving Individual Gold Medal at the FEI Pony Driving World Championships. He was the first equine from the United States to win such an award.

A Modern American Shetland Pony
stands for a conformation photo.
In addition to exhibiting typical pony
characteristics, such as a shorter
leg-to-body ratio, compact build,
and attractive head, the Modern
American Shetland shown here could
excel in any number of pony activities,
from a children's pony to an adult's
driving animal.

While they are mainly noted for their success in the English pleasure and pony hunter rings, Welsh Ponies (Section B) can also do very well in many other disciplines, such as carriage driving. Here a Section B uses its natural athletic abilities to navigate a cones course at a breed show.

The Welsh Pony (Section B) is the most refined of the four Welsh sections. Well known as children's riding and hunter ponies, the Section B excels at English riding events and in the hunter ring. Beautiful heads, superb movement, good temperaments, and athletic ability are typical of the Section B ponies. This two-year-old grey colt exhibits the free and reaching movement that is admired in the Welsh breed.

A handsome Dales Pony stallion canters across his field and exhibits the typical characteristics of his breed: a powerful build, muscular body, and ample bone. Dales Ponies are also noted for their strength and stamina and are usually the black or dark brown color shown here. When full grown, Dales Ponies stand an average of 14.2 hands tall.

LIGHT HORSES

Warmbloods are the ultimate in elegance, power, athleticism, grace, and beauty. All of these attributes are displayed in the Danish Warmblood gelding shown here exhibiting his beautiful cadenced canter.

Moving on up from the pony breeds, we arrive at the most populous type of horses: the light horse breeds. The light horses are larger than ponies but smaller than the draft breeds. Light horses typically range from 14.2 to 16 hands, although many light horses fall outside of those height parameters. Average weights for light horses fall in the range of 800 to 1,200 pounds. Light horses are beautiful, graceful animals that are full of refinement, endurance, and athleticism. They possess more spirit and animation than is generally found in the heavier horse breeds. The light horse breeds are usually what people have in mind when they think of a horse. Light horses are used for an enormously wide range of purposes, from quiet jobs like family horses, pleasure mounts, and trail horses to much more demanding disciplines such as show horses, endurance riding, eventing, dressage, racing, and jumping.

There are far more light horses in the world than drafts or ponies, due in part to the sheer popularity of breeds like the Quarter Horse, Thoroughbred, Arabian, and others. However, not every light horse breed is common or well known. For instance, the Cleveland Bay has become quite rare over the years, while other breeds are popular only within a small group of enthusiasts and remain obscure to the general public. A specific breed might gain a reputation for being well-suited to only one particular discipline and may lose potential

Some of the most famous horses in American history have been Thoroughbreds; from the great Man o' War to the incomparable Secretariat. There is no other breed that has gained such widespread fame.

owners who are not interested in that sport or aspect of riding or driving. This is unfortunate because, as we will see, so many of these light horse breeds are extremely versatile and can perform many tasks. Often it is simply a matter of the right training, which can be much more influential than merely following what a breed was bred to do.

Light horses come in a wide range of physical appearances with enough variety to suit anyone. Most light breeds have pleasing,

Two Missouri Fox Trotting Horses graze peacefully in their Florida pasture. Black and chestnut varieties are shown here, but the breed can also be found in a variety of solid coat colors, as well as pinto patterns. Only Appaloosa-type markings are discouraged.

attractive heads, and avoid the extremes of the bowed Roman nose of the draft breeds or the intensely compact cute faces of ponies. Individual appearances can vary greatly within the light horse breeds. From the refined, athletic, and energetic breeds such as Arabian and Thoroughbred, the indispensable Quarter Horse, the powerful substance of the Warmblood breeds, and the smooth gaited movements of the American Saddlebred and Missouri Fox Trotting Horse, there is truly a light horse breed out there able to achieve any task you may desire. Let's take a closer look at some of the light horses.

Any discussion of light horses must inevitably begin with the Arabian. Exquisite in its beauty, the Arabian is a delight to the eye. It is an ancient breed that has fascinated horse lovers for centuries. Characterized by its gorgeous, dished face and huge eyes, the Arabian is also noted for its endurance and versatility. One of the purest of all horse breeds, the Arabian originated in Asia, although sources do not agree on an exact country of origin. Arabians are tremendously popular for their beauty and qualities of athleticism and stamina.

The American Quarter Horse is the most popular breed of horse in America and has entirely eclipsed all other breeds in terms of sheer numbers and registrations. This is an important testament to the breed's excellent characteristics,

The Arabian breed exudes a mystical charm and has a universal appeal, which has been undoubtedly increased by the enormous popularity of Walter Farley's classic horse story *The Black Stallion*. The second book in the series, *The Black Stallion Returns,* features an exciting race across the Arabian desert.

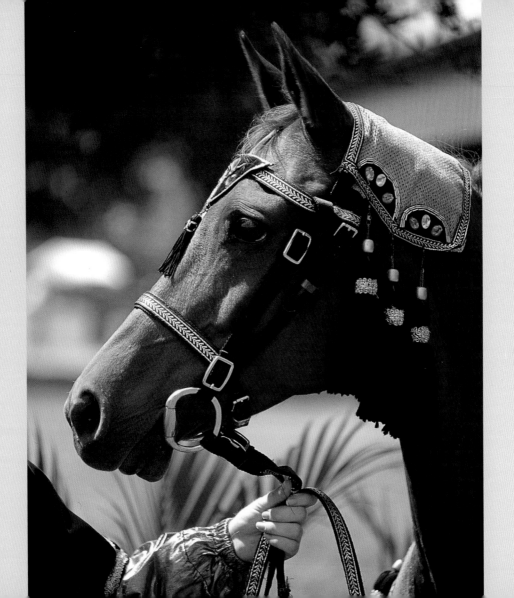

including a calm and pleasant demeanor and an impressive versatility. Initially influenced by Spanish horses, the Quarter Horse was later influenced by the Thoroughbred. Quarter Horses are enormously popular in Western disciplines, but they are also very talented in other spheres. The name "Quarter Horse" comes from early American racing when horses were matched against each other over short distances. The American Quarter Horse is still the fastest animal in the world at quarter-mile racing. They are the ultimate all-around family horse.

Best known as the world's premier racing breed, the Thoroughbred has a long and fascinating history. Developed in England, the breed's main foundation lines were Spanish and Arabian via three important stallions: The Darley Arabian, The Godolphin Arabian, and The Byerly Turk. In fact, all purebred Thoroughbreds of today are said to descend from at least one of these lines. Although their prominent use is racing, it would be impossible to overlook the Thoroughbred's talent in many other equestrian disciplines, including dressage, jumping, and eventing. The Thoroughbred is immensely popular all over the world and possesses athleticism and quality. The popularity of recent movies such as *Seabiscuit* and *Dreamer* shows that horse racing still captures people's imaginations.

Few breeds can trace their entire history back to one specific stallion, but the Morgan is a notable exception. A dark bay stallion named Figure, a prepotent

A Warmblood performs an FEI Grand Prix dressage test. Dressage is an exciting and beautiful sport to watch, particularly at its highest levels. Complicated movements appear fluid and effortless, and the rider's aids are almost impossible to detect, which makes the horse and rider appear in perfect harmony.

individual of approximately 14 hands, was later renamed after the stallion's owner, Justin Morgan. The name Justin Morgan gave way to the name of the breed—the Morgan. While the Morgan's heritage remains a mystery, some believe that the original Justin Morgan may have been influenced by Welsh Cobs, Thoroughbreds, Friesians, and Arabians. Today the Morgan is a beautiful breed with substance and quality and is well-suited to a variety of disciplines.

The Morgan is used in many types of equestrian activities, including hunt seat riding, saddle seat, dressage, and Western disciplines, as well as driving and long-distance and endurance riding. Of course they also make wonderful family horses and companions.

The ultimate harness racing horse is the Standardbred. Its name refers to the standard speed that horses originally needed to achieve in order to be registered in the stud book. Like the Morgan, the Standardbred breed is heavily influenced by a single specific foundation stallion. In the case of the Standardbred, this stallion was named Hambletonian 10 and he sired over 1,300 offspring. Hambletonian 10 was a grandson of the breed's initial foundation sire, Messenger, who was a Thoroughbred. Today, Hambletonian 10 is remembered each year during the annual running of the Hambletonian, a prestigious race for three-year-old Standardbreds.

The Andalusian is an ancient breed of Spanish origin and is an impressive animal with substance and quality. They are particularly noted for their quiet temperaments and fabulous action. Andalusians are often grey, although other colors are acceptable. The breed is said to have influenced a multitude of other breeds, from the American Quarter Horse to the Friesian and beyond.

Rapidly gaining popularity in the United States, the Friesian is easily recognizable due to its striking black coloring and abundant feathering. The Friesian is an ancient breed that was initially influenced by the Forest horse in the Netherlands and has in turn influenced other breeds such as the Fell Pony and the Dales Pony. Friesians are always black. White markings are prohibited with the exception of a tiny star.

A string of fresh ribbons blows in the breeze at a horse show and is the reward for which all competitors strive. While open horse shows allow entries from horses or ponies of any breed, there are also breed-specific shows where exhibitors compete only against other horses of the same breed.

Although they are currently very rare in the United States (the American Livestock Breeds Conservancy has designated the breed as critical on its 2007 Conservation Priority List, which means less than 50 are registered annually in the United States), the Cleveland Bay has a long history. The Cleveland Bay Horse Society has been in existence in England since 1884. The breed has historically been a very popular carriage horse, and they are always bay as their name implies. White markings are not allowed except for a small star.

The Mustang, in all of its rugged charm, completely embodies the spirit of the American West. Descending from the original Spanish horses that were imported to America many centuries ago, the Mustangs of today still retain much of their original Spanish type. While many Mustangs still roam free in the western states, others have been adopted by private owners through the Bureau of Land Management's adoption program.

One of the most unique light horses is the North American Curly Horse (also known as the American Bashkir Curly Horse). The origin of curly horses is unknown but some believe that the first curly-coated horses were found in the Bashkir region of Russia. Curly horses feature distinctive curly-haired coats that are strikingly unusual when compared to the coat of a typical horse. Curly horses

A very unique type of coat is found on the North American Curly Horse, also known as the American Bashkir Curly Horse. Its distinctive coat is curly and it has been found that some people who are allergic to horses can sometimes be around curly horses without suffering from their usual symptoms. For this reason they are sometimes called hypoallergenic horses.

are currently considered a coat type rather than a breed. Research is being undertaken to determine the genetic reasons for the curly coat type and to better understand the inheritance of curly coats. Curly horses are found in all colors and are noted for their kind dispositions and overall versatility.

The perennial popularity of the Arabian has also given way to a couple of popular Arabian crossbreeds: the Anglo-Arab and the Morab. The Anglo-Arab originated through the crossbreeding of Thoroughbreds and Arabians. This is an extremely popular breed in France, although they are also popular in many other countries as well. Ideally, the breed is an excellent combination of the characteristics of the Arabian and the Thoroughbred, representing the positive qualities of both breeds in one talented and athletic package. The fact that Anglo-Arabs are attractive and eye-catching comes as no surprise, given this background. Like the Anglo-Arab, the Morab was developed with a specific purpose in mind: to accentuate and consolidate the excellent characteristics of the Arabian and the Morgan in one breed. The name Morab is credited to William Randolph Hearst, who was an avid Morab breeder. The breed is noted for its beauty and quality, and is a popular choice for many disciplines, which is not surprising when you consider the popularity of its parent breeds.

This handsome Latvian gelding exhibits a kind expression and soft eye that illustrates the breed's pleasant demeanor.

WARMBLOODS

As a group, the Warmblood breeds are very popular in the United States as sport horses because they are typically well suited to equestrian disciplines, such as dressage, eventing, and show jumping. Although each breed of Warmblood is slightly different in terms of its type and development, they are all generally descended from similar foundation breeds with their names typically indicating their country of origin.

As the name reveals, the Swedish Warmblood was developed in Sweden during the 1600s. The list of influential breeds is quite extensive and ranges from Spanish horses to Friesians, Arabians, and Trakehners. With more than 350 years of careful breeding, the Swedish Warmblood has become a horse with a very consistent and specific type well suited for many equestrian sports ranging from dressage to driving.

The Danish Warmblood Registry was established in Denmark in the 1960s, which makes it one of the more recently developed Warmblood types in Europe. The foundation breeds of the Danish Warmblood include two of Denmark's older horse breeds: the Frederiksborg and the Holsteiner. The Danish Warmblood was also influenced by the Thoroughbred. Unlike many of the other Warmblood breeds, the Danish Warmblood has no Hanoverian blood, which has given it a more distinctive look than some of the other Warmbloods.

An aged Icelandic stallion canters by and shows off his thick and beautiful mane as it flows in the breeze. Icelandics are a notably hardy breed with long life expectancies.

Like its cousins the Swedish Warmblood and Danish Warmblood, the Dutch Warmblood is an athletic and talented sport horse. It is very popular for dressage and jumping. The Dutch Warmblood descends from two historic Dutch breeds, the Gelderlender and the Groningen, and was also influenced by infusions of Thoroughbred blood. This breed has a reputation for quality and excellence.

Particularly noted for its talent in show jumping, the Selle Francais is a French Warmblood that was founded upon native Norman horses that were crossed mainly with Arabians, Anglo-Arabs, and Thoroughbreds, as well as French Trotters. The breed is known in France as *Le Cheval de Selle Francais*, which translates to "the French saddle horse." The breed is an elegant one with a proven record as a sport horse.

While the American Warmblood doesn't have the lengthy history that some of the other Warmbloods have, it is founded upon many of the same ideals that have made Warmbloods in general so popular. American Warmbloods are not always completely consistent in type, but they are popular and their usefulness in equine sport is impressive.

The sport of dressage (*dressage* is the French word for training) truly affects all other aspects of riding. No matter what discipline the rider may choose to focus on, the wisest equestrians always keep a close eye on their dressage basics. The Warmblood pictured here is competing at a high level of the sport and demonstrates what is possible with the right effort and training.

The Trakehner is a Warmblood of quality and beauty and is currently very popular in dressage and eventing. Developed centuries ago in the former country of East Prussia, the Trakehner breed was founded from native Schweiken horses that were selectively crossed with Thoroughbreds and Arabians. The result is a slightly more refined type than some of the other Warmblood breeds.

Three Western pleasure competitors await the announcement of the class winner over the loudspeaker. Here we have an interesting example of three unique colors in one class: a chestnut-and-white American Paint Horse, a solid chestnut American Quarter Horse, and a bay American Quarter Horse.

Although it was originally developed as an outstanding carriage horse, the Oldenburg's current claim to fame is its excellence under saddle. The breed was initially developed during the seventeenth century by the Count of Oldenburg in Germany. The foundation breeds included the Friesian, Thoroughbred, and Norfolk Roadster. Today the Oldenburg is a popular breed well suited for dressage.

Named for its place of origin—Latvia—the Latvian breed is a bit more unusual in America than some of the other sport horse breeds. The Latvian was developed during the first half of the twentieth century and greatly influenced by the Oldenburg along with other breeds, such as the Hanoverian. There are said to be three types of Latvians: the Latvian draft horse, the Latvian harness horse, and the lightweight Latvian. The latter has the most influence from Thoroughbreds and Hanoverians.

GAITED HORSES

All horses have gaits, which are varying types of movement such as the four-beat walk, the two-beat trot, the three-beat canter, and the four-beat gallop. Gaited horses are unique in the fact that they have differing gaits from the traditional walk, trot, canter, and gallop typically found in light horse breeds. From the Icelandic's unique *tölt* and the Missouri Fox Trotting Horse's fox trot to the rhythmic and smooth running walk of the Tennessee Walking Horse, these gaits are what make our next group of horses particularly distinctive.

While the name insinuates an origin in the Rocky Mountains of western North America, it is interesting to discover that the Rocky Mountain Horse was actually developed in Kentucky during the first half of the twentieth century.

A Paso Fino horse and rider compete in a horse show wearing traditional show attire. The name "Paso Fino" is actually a shortened version of the original Spanish name *Los Caballos de Paso Fino*, which means "the horses with the fine walk." Today, the fine walk is a treasured attribute of this lovely gaited breed.

The breed's name derives from one stallion, Old Tobe, who was brought to Kentucky and was said to have come from the Rocky Mountains. Local horse owners began calling him the "Rocky Mountain horse" and it was the beginning of what is now a popular gaited breed made famous by the breed's popular four-beat single-foot gait.

Two grey Thoroughbred mares graze near a pond. In the United States, the Thoroughbred is often closely associated with three prestigious spring races: the Kentucky Derby, the Preakness Stakes, and the Belmont Stakes. All three races are for three-year-olds, are set at grueling distances, and take place in the span of only five weeks. These historic races have been run for more than 130 years, but the newer Breeders' Cup series is also gaining popularity.

Rocky Mountain Horses are particularly noted for their kind temperaments.

Well-known for its kind and pleasant disposition, the Tennessee Walking Horse is noted for its three gaits: the flat-footed walk, the running walk, and the rocking chair canter. All are extremely smooth gaits and very easy to ride. The background of the Tennessee Walking Horse is a mixture of many popular breeds, including the Thoroughbred,

Horses are very social animals and have a desire to be around other animals. They have very strong herd instincts and feel safer when surrounded by their companions. These good neighbors (two Friesians and an American Paint Horse) chat across the fence.

Morgan, Saddlebred, and Standardbred, as well as some Narragansett Pacer blood. The breed's foundation stallion, Black Allen, was born in the 1880s and was produced from crossing a Standardbred and a Morgan. Black Allen is credited with great influence on the Tennessee Walking Horse breed.

The American Saddlebred is another very popular gaited breed that was developed during the nineteenth century in Kentucky. The breed descends from the Narragansett Pacer and has influence from the Thoroughbred and Morgan horses. Today, the American Saddlebred is one of the top ten breeds in America. It is often seen in the show ring demonstrating its five gaits: walk, trot, canter, slow gait, and rack. The breed is elegant and eye catching, accentuated by an attractive head.

Although it is pony-sized, the Icelandic is considered a horse because its characteristics are more horse-like than pony-like. The Icelandic is somewhat unique among horse breeds in that the horses were bred in Iceland without outside influence from other breeds for nearly a thousand years and are free from any type of crossbreeding. Icelandics are notably long-lived and very hardy, which is a result of centuries of survival against the harsh Icelandic weather conditions. It is a gaited breed with five gaits, including the distinctive *tölt,* which is a type of running walk.

This Anglo-Arab is competing in a hunter class at a show. A combination of Arabian and Thoroughbred breeding, the Anglo-Arab blends the Arabian's endurance with the Thoroughbred's athleticism, which ideally results in a horse that displays the most positive characteristics of each breed. There are nearly 10,000 Anglo-Arabs registered with the Arabian Horse Association.

Considered by many to be the ultimate choice for trail and pleasure riding, the Missouri Fox Trotting Horse (or Missouri Fox Trotter) is immensely popular in those realms. The Missouri Fox Trotting Horse possesses a unique gait known as the fox trot, as well as the flat-footed walk and a rocking horse canter. As the name indicates, the breed was developed in the Ozarks of Missouri. The Missouri Fox Trotting Horse Breeders' Association was founded in 1948.

The Paso Fino has its own distinct set of gaits that are prized for their smoothness. These include the *paso fino* (equivalent to a walk), the *paso corto* (equivalent to a trot), and the *paso largo* (equivalent to a canter). The Paso Fino is of Puerto Rican origin and is believed to have been influenced by the Andalusian and Spanish Jennet. The Paso Fino exhibits the characteristics of its Spanish heritage and is a moderately small horse that usually stands under 15 hands.

Although their names are similar, the Peruvian Paso is not directly related to the Paso Fino. They are distinctly different breeds that happen to share the Paso name. Peruvian Pasos were developed in Peru and were bred from a mixture of Spanish Jennet, Andalusian, Barb, and Friesian blood. Like the Paso Fino, the Peruvian Paso is a gaited breed and is popular for trail and pleasure riding. The Peruvian Paso's gaits include the walk, Paso Llano, and Sobreandando.

A lovely young Morgan mare gallops across a grassy field. The Morgan is smaller than some of the other light horse breeds, with most individuals standing between 14.2 and 15.2 hands. Some even stay within pony height at under 14.2 hands.

This American Saddlebred makes a wonderful family horse thanks to his kind disposition, versatility, and willing attitude. These admirable characteristics are beneficial in encouraging and fueling the horsey interests of children who may have outgrown their first pony and are ready to take on the care of a larger animal.

An American Quarter Horse in Western tack prepares to enter its next event during a rodeo. The Quarter Horse has been a staple of rodeos in the United States for years and continues to be the horse of choice for millions of riders worldwide.

Opposite: Just look at that gorgeous face! A curious Arabian peers out from the window of his stall. The Arabian is well known for its beautiful, sculpted head set on an equally elegant neck and body.

The Swedish Warmblood is a beautiful animal with talent to match its appearance. Swedish Warmbloods have been enormously successful in sport horse disciplines and have garnered many Olympic medals in equestrian sports.

The Missouri Fox Trotting Horse averages 14 to 16 hands. The breed is prized by owners and riders for its smooth gaits, particularly the fox trot from which the breed gets its name. Missouri Fox Trotting Horses are found in a rainbow of colors, both in solid and pinto (as shown here).

A young and attractive Standardbred
stallion stands for a conformation
photograph. The Standardbred averages
a height of 15.2 hands, although
individuals can be found on either side
of this average. The breed has a similar
appearance to the related Thoroughbred
and is generally considered a quiet,
people-oriented horse.

The Latvian, a type of Warmblood, exhibits many of the characteristics that have made Warmbloods so popular—power, poise, and general athletic abilities. Here, an eye-catching Latvian gelding gallops across the pasture.

Opposite: This elegant, athletic, and powerful Oldenburg gallops through his paddock on a perfect autumn afternoon. Warmbloods are generally strong and versatile creatures. They are typically calmer and can be easier to train than some of the other more temperamental horse breeds.

The Tennessee Walking Horse is well-loved for its quiet temperament, which makes it a good choice as a first horse for beginning riders and handlers. The Tennessee Walking Horse usually stands between 15 and 16.2 hands.

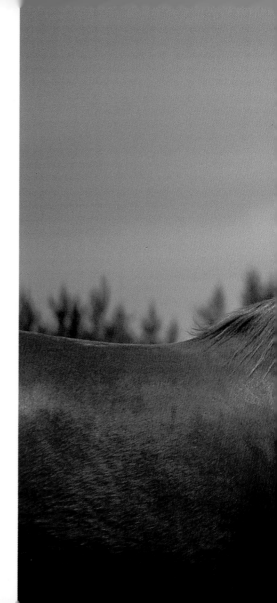

A beautiful Morgan prepares for the saddleseat equitation class at a horse show. Saddleseat riding is a specific style of English riding that is different from the more commonly seen hunt seat or dressage. In saddleseat, one of the rider's main goals is to show off the extravagant action of their mount, particularly at the trot.

Opposite: Unlike Appendix Quarter Horses (a Quarter Horse with Thoroughbred blood), the basis of the Foundation Quarter Horse is focused heavily upon the original type of American Quarter Horse, as seen prior to the infusion of the Thoroughbred influence. Today many breeders specialize in Foundation Quarter Horses and seek to ensure the original breed type is preserved.

A staple of the Western pleasure class is the American Quarter Horse. The energetic walk, relaxed jog, and collected lope that is found so often in this breed makes it the first choice of many riders who wish to compete in this aspect of showing. Here a relaxed Quarter Horse makes its way about the arena while the judge looks on in the background.

Left: This Hanoverian, formerly a successful upper-level dressage horse, spends the days of his retirement bringing joy and entertainment to others during an autumn equestrian demonstration.

Opposite: The tools of the trade are a Western saddle and bridle as seen on the back of an American Quarter Horse. Western tack is designed with comfort and beauty in mind, as well as practical function.

A dressage drill team completes the finale of their annual demonstration. Although these horses are of many different breeds, they have spent months working together as a team to present a breathtaking and amazing performance.

A black Trakehner warms up before a dressage test. Trakehners can be found competing at the highest levels of this sport, as well as other events such as show jumping.

The Morgan is a strong, versatile, and athletic breed capable of performing any number of tasks, both under saddle and in harness. Add the Morgan's natural good looks and fine conformation into the equation and you have a remarkable all-around breed.

This compact and agile Thoroughbred comes to a graceful sliding stop and kicks up a cloud of dust. The Thoroughbred is typically a large breed and usually reaches heights of 15.2 to 17 hands.

A saddle bronc attempts to unseat its rider during a rodeo competition. The horses used for these events are not any particular breed and are not wild horses. They are simply horses that have a knack for bucking.

Opposite: The Trakehner has a well-shaped, attractive head, which is a sign of the breed's Thoroughbred influence. Care has been taken to maintain the Trakehner's original type, and only occasionally have Thoroughbred and Arabian blood been introduced during the breed's development.

A young Rocky Mountain Horse foal watches some of the other members of his herd from across the pasture. Notice the darker color beginning to show along the foal's muzzle. This is the true color that he will become after shedding out his much lighter baby coat.

This is not a trail drive or a scene from a Western movie. It is just a large herd of horses enjoying themselves by racing across a field and giving us a good opportunity to see several light horse breeds at once. This herd includes some Appaloosas, a few Tennessee Walking Horses, and a handful of American Quarter Horses, among others.

Opposite: The lovely details of this Western bridle nicely accentuate the beauty of the Arabian head. Arabians have many distinguishing characteristics, but probably the most notable is their exotically beautiful head. They have large, liquid eyes set prominently on the sides of the face; a dished (concave) profile that tapers down to a tiny muzzle; well-set ears; and flaring nostrils. It is a picture-perfect head brimming with beauty.

A bay Morgan and chestnut Haflinger share a quiet moment together at the edge of the herd. By viewing both breeds together, it's easy to see that this Haflinger has a stockier, more substantial build than this Morgan, who is slightly more refined. Because of this, however, the Morgan has the advantage of a more attractive face.

Show time! Two American Quarter Horses munch on a snack of hay while waiting to unload for an exciting day of showing. With luck, these two pals might come home with blue ribbons.

Opposite: The Arabian Horse Association has developed a Discovery Farm program that allows interested horse enthusiasts to visit participating Arabian farms, giving them the opportunity to get acquainted with and learn more about the breed in a hands-on format. There are over 600 Discovery Farms nationwide.

Two gorgeous Latvians display all of the qualities that the breed is known for. Although Latvians are Warmbloods in type and by blood, they are not called Latvian Warmbloods.

An American Quarter Horse takes careful aim and successfully makes the tight turns of a barrel race at high speed. The Quarter Horse has undoubtedly proven its skill in such events. Quick maneuverability combined with fast acceleration and complete obedience result in an excellent choice for barrel racing.

A spirited Icelandic horse stallion races into view. Icelandic horses are a gaited breed, and some individuals have the ability to perform five different gaits: walk, trot, canter, *tölt*, and *skei*.

He may be a Tennessee Walking Horse, but this gelding certainly isn't walking! The Tennessee Walking Horse Breeders and Exhibitors Association, which provides the registry for the breed, closed its stud book in 1947. This means that the breed has not accepted infusions of outside breeding into purebred Tennessee Walking Horses for more than 60 years.

This athletic and energetic Appendix Quarter Horse makes a bold and brave leap over a fence. The Appendix Quarter Horse combines some of the best aspects and talents of the American Quarter Horse and Thoroughbred to create a swift and sound horse.

The Missouri Fox Trotting Horse Breed Association's motto is "every rider's pleasure horse," and this is a testament to the gaited breed's excellence as a trail and pleasure mount. The distinctive fox trot is essentially performed by the horse's ability to walk with its front legs and trot with its hind legs.

A palomino
American Quarter
Horse poses in
fancy Western gear.
Silver-appointed
saddles, bridles,
and halters are
favored by
enthusiasts of
stock-type
breeds, such
as the American
Quarter Horse.

Two Morab horses stand peacefully together in the early morning light. The Morab, a popular Morgan-Arabian cross, has been in existence since the 1800s, but the breed's registry was not established until the 1970s.

Somewhat smaller than the Peruvian Paso, the average Paso Fino stands less than 15 hands. Its gaits include the *paso fino*, the *paso corto*, and the *paso largo*.

Here a black Trakehner canters alongside a Cleveland Bay. The Trakehner breed is named for the farm where the original Trakehner horses were bred, which was in Trakehnen, East Prussia. The Cleveland Bay was originally known as the Chapman, but the name was changed to reflect the area where the breed originated.

Bold, beautiful, and black! The Friesian registry was opened in 1879, and all Friesians of today are said to descend from a single original stallion.

Opposite: A pretty grey Arabian strikes a classic halter pose. Arabians are not particularly large horses, with most examples standing in the 14.1- to 15.1-hand range.

The Arabian has been used as a cross with many breeds to complement them and add beauty, elegance, and stamina to the mix. This is a Dutch Warmblood-Arabian cross gelding demonstrating the wonderful results that can be achieved through Arabian crossbreeding.

A bay Morgan grazes alongside a palomino American Quarter Horse gelding while crisp autumn colors glow in the background. Both of these breeds make terrific family horses due to their calm natures and great versatility.

Thoroughbreds, American Paint Horses, and Warmbloods compete together in an English pleasure class at a horse show.

Opposite: A rider on a Thoroughbred enters the ring for a hunter class. The first Thoroughbred in America was named Bulle Rock, and he was a son of the Darley Arabian. Bulle Rock was imported to the United States in 1730.

Time to cool off! This grey Thoroughbred is enjoying a quick swim. The grey coloring in the Thoroughbred breed is credited to a single stallion, Alcock's Arabian, from 1700.

An attractive Cleveland Bay mare poses for a head portrait. Other than the British native ponies, the Cleveland Bay is Britain's oldest equine breed. It is said to be critically endangered in both the United States and the United Kingdom.

A large field of Standardbreds race for the finish line during a harness race at a local county fair circuit. Harness racing has a long and interesting history, and the Standardbred breed was developed specifically for the purpose of racing in this venue.

Opposite: An early morning mist rises behind this pair of horses. It is a beautiful scene to the eyes of any horse lover. Grazing in this picturesque field are an American Paint Horse and a black Morgan.

A happy American Quarter Horse owner gives her horse a nice pat after a class. The Quarter Horse is commonly seen competing in all areas of Western riding and is often seen at various levels of local, 4-H, and breed shows.

An American Quarter Horse charges into camera view. The breed's name is derived from the short distances (such as the quarter mile) it can cover at tremendous speed. Quarter Horse racing is still an exciting and competitive sport today, although the breed is more well known for its abilities as a good working animal and family mount.

The breed's Spanish influence is particularly evident in this Peruvian Paso's face. The breed is often confused with the similarly named Paso Fino, but the two breeds are quite distinct. They were developed independently of each other in different countries.

One size doesn't fit all. In the world of equine breeds, there is a horse, pony, or mule to suit the needs of any horse owner. Sometimes it just takes time to find the right horse. Here a Pinto peeks over his shoulder in the midst of the herd.

Opposite: This grey American Warmblood canters into a turn during a hunter class at a show. Some American Warmbloods have draft horse breeding in their backgrounds, while others are bred from the more traditional Warmblood breeds.

The Tennessee Walking Horse is a gaited breed, well loved for the smoothness of its ride. Famous for its four-beat running walk, which the breed naturally possesses, the Tennessee Walking Horse is praised by trail riders and show riders alike and is recommended for any rider wishing to cover a long distance in comfort.

A Rocky Mountain Horse poses for a head and neck portrait. The attractive face of a Rocky Mountain Horse is one of the many qualities that have endeared it to enthusiasts for decades. The breed's registry was founded during the mid-1980s.

Missouri Fox Trotting Horses graze along the fence lines of this lovely facility. The Missouri Fox Trotting Horse is highly prized for its smooth gaits and comfortable ride, which makes it the breed of choice for many trail and pleasure riders.

Opposite: A beautiful bay Arabian gelding canters across his pasture. Arabians are the only horse breed to feature 15 skeletal vertebrae instead of the 16 vertebrae possessed by most horses. This typically results in a shorter back. Arabians also have a characteristically flat croup with high tail carriage.

This attractive Icelandic stallion with his full, flowing mane and beautiful movement is a lovely representative of his breed. Despite its small stature (most Icelandics reach only 12.3 to 13.2 hands), the breed is considered to be a horse and not a pony because the Icelandic language does not have a word for pony. Another reason is because they are the only equines on the island and the differentiation isn't needed.

Previous spread, right:
These two grey
Thoroughbreds are a
little unusual. Darker
colors are more
commonly seen
throughout the breed.
Many people make the
error of calling a grey
horse "white," when
in fact a truly white
Thoroughbred is very
rare and seldom seen.

The well-shaped,
attractive face of this
Hanoverian peers out
the window of her stall
and shows us her
intelligent expression.
The Hanoverian stands
at an average of
16.2 hands.

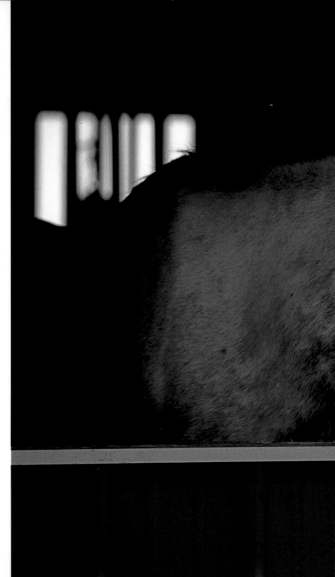

A small herd of four horses enjoys a quiet morning in the sunlight. It is a beautiful sight, no matter what breed.

A beautiful Latvian mare charges
ahead at full speed. Most Latvians are
found in dark colors, such as this bay,
and are also black and brown.

This is an up-close view of the amusing ringlets in the forelock and mane of a young American Bashkir Curly Horse foal. Just as the breed's coats curl, so do their manes and tails.

Opposite: The ideal American Quarter Horse will have a small and well-shaped head with a broad forehead and kind eyes set on a muscular, well-shaped neck. This horse is an excellent example.

The Warmbloods in this dressage drill team display some common dressage techniques and present them in an entertaining and unique way. Because this drill team is performing at a charity benefit event, they have added to the spectator appeal by wearing fun costumes.

Opposite: The athletic and elegant Hanoverian is a popular sport horse. This Warmblood breed originated in Germany and is well-known for its abilities as a show jumper and dressage horse.

A lovely American Saddlebred relaxes at home in his pasture. The American Saddlebred is known for its pleasant disposition, which makes it a fine choice for many equestrians. The breed makes a wonderful riding and fine harness animal.

The Selle Francais is a French breed that is known for its superb jumping ability and is also noted for its talent in the dressage ring. The breed has been influenced by Thoroughbreds and Arabians and possesses a trainable mind and an easy-going temperament. This bay gelding canters effortlessly across his paddock.

Opposite: A breeding stock American Paint Horse grazes with its pasture mate. Minimally marked American Paint Horses are designated as breeding stock because they possess the type and characteristics desired in the breed and are valuable breeding animals, despite their lack of color.

Reining is quickly becoming an extremely popular sport and has a huge following. Here a well turned-out American Quarter Horse and rider prepare for a sliding stop, one of the sport's exciting maneuvers.

A handsome Latvian gelding blows "steam" after playing hard during turnout on a cool fall morning. The Rheinland Pfalz-Saar International organization inspects and registers Latvians, along with many other sport-type horse and pony breeds.

A gorgeous Swedish Warmblood
mare charges past the camera and
shows us her elegant, refined head;
expressive eyes; and kind expression.
Swedish Warmbloods usually reach
a height of around 16.2 hands.

This Rocky Mountain Horse displays the breed's signature color: a combination of a chocolate coat and a flaxen mane and tail. This has become the color combo most desired by breeders of Rocky Mountain Horses. Although any solid color is perfectly acceptable, high white stockings on the legs are discouraged.

Opposite: An adorable American Bashkir Curly Horse foal is featured in this portrait. These horses are found in all colors including buckskin, as pictured here. The unique curls are most prominent during the winter months when the horses' coats are at their longest.

These four horses watch the daily barn activities from across this pond during the foggy tranquility of early morning. It is a beautiful scene sure to please the eye of those who admire equines of all types and breeds.

The Thoroughbred is well-known to horse lovers as a racing animal, and millions follow the excitement of Thoroughbred racing all over the world. This gelding is a grandson of the incredible Thoroughbred stallion Storm Cat, who has produced numerous race winners.

Although this gelding is a purebred Arabian, there is also a slightly different breed that is known as a Shagya Arabian. The Shagya Arabian is not considered to be a purebred Arabian because it carries some outside blood, including Spanish and Thoroughbred. The breed's foundation sire was named Shagya, which is why the breed came to be known as Shagya Arabian.

A brave and bold Thoroughbred takes aim at a fence during a hunter class and clears the obstacle with room to spare. With its talent, elegance, and beauty, Thoroughbreds are well suited to many English riding events such as these.

There is enough action and excitement for everyone at a rodeo. Here, two American Quarter Horses race across the arena in pursuit of a calf during a calf-roping event.

Opposite: Some horse registries require that their horses be branded upon registration to ensure proper identification later on. Other breeds forego this formality altogether. For instance, Thoroughbreds are given a lip tattoo with an identification number that tells the horse's year of birth.

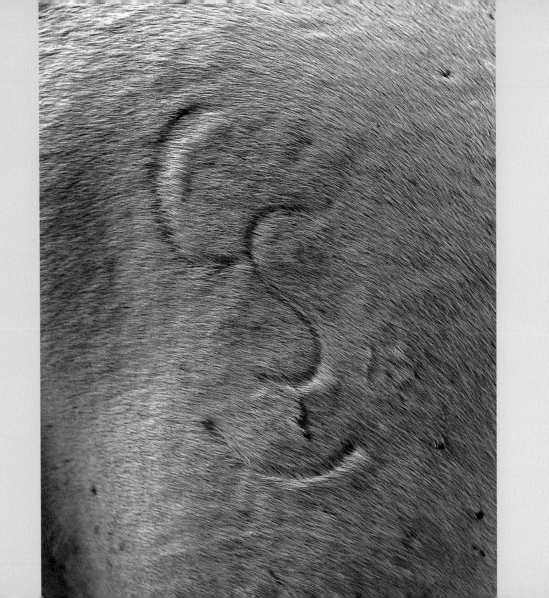

The Cleveland Bay is always bay, as the name implies. No white markings on the legs are permitted and only a small white star on the forehead is allowed on the face. However, in a more recent effort to help preserve the rare breed, individuals who exhibit more white than usual are still eligible for registration as long as a notation is made in the studbook that this particular horse exhibits more white than usual.

Opposite: A dressage rider astride a Latvian mare completes a training-level dressage test. Dressage is a sport with a place for every horse and rider, ranging from novices to extremely advanced riders. Warmbloods excel in dressage worldwide.

A group of horses of various breeds, types, and colors graze on the hills in late fall. It is a picturesque sight and one that will surely thrill the heart of any horse lover.

Handsome and well-balanced, this chestnut Arabian gelding has achieved great success in the show ring and has won classes both in-hand and under saddle. Many Arabian owners are very involved with showing their horses at Arabian breed shows.

American Quarter Horses have long been used as ranch horses and perform all sorts of tasks from the herding and cutting of cattle to trail drives and general riding. While the breed's natural versatility has made it popular for all kinds of disciplines, the American Quarter Horse is still a popular choice for performing these types of ranch chores.

The American Quarter Horse is said to have natural "cow sense." This natural trait, coupled with the proper time and training, results in a dependable and extremely intelligent animal. Here an American Quarter Horse holds a calf steady during a rodeo event.

Two young riders take to the wooded trails astride a pair of American Quarter Horses. The height of this breed can vary considerably depending on the individual's specific type. With some of the smaller and more compact Quarter Horses standing only a little over pony height of 14.2 hands, they can make wonderful all-around family horses for novices or beginners who might be intimidated by a larger animal. This, along with the breed's calm and willing attitude, makes them a great children's horse.

An American Quarter Horse waits patiently for the return of his handler while tied to a trailer. The American Quarter Horse is the most popular breed in the United States and possibly the world. Over 160,000 foals were registered with the American Quarter Horse Association in 2005 alone.

Opposite: Warmbloods excel in all types of English riding events and at all levels. With the large selection of Warmblood breeds available, there certainly is a type for every rider.

A black Rocky Mountain Horse gallops along a fence line, fresh from being let out of the barn on a cool summer's evening. Comfortable to ride, with smooth, fluid gaits, the Rocky Mountain Horse is also a sound and sure-footed animal that is popular with long-distance and pleasure riders.

Opposite: The American Saddlebred has always been a very popular show horse, with its high-stepping action and attractive head. It is probably one of the most well-known gaited breeds.

An aged grey Arabian pauses to drink from a stream. As one of the main foundation breeds for the Thoroughbred, it's easy to see similarities in structure between the two breeds.

Although Arabians are found in many colors, grey is one of the most classic. Many of the breed's foundation stallions, including the incomparable Raffles and Skowronek, have been grey. Here a lovely grey Arabian strikes a pose during a halter class.

Opposite: An attractive bay Thoroughbred gelding poses for a quick portrait. The ideal Thoroughbred should be well-muscled, have a sleek coat, and possess a lovely, refined head set on a graceful neck. The Thoroughbred is an athletic, powerful, spirited, and beautiful breed that is capable of reaching speeds approaching 45 miles per hour. While some individuals can be quiet and calm to work around and ride, other Thoroughbreds may have an intense or easily excitable nature.

Wild horses are found throughout North America. The Mustang is found in the west, and the famous Chincoteague Ponies and lesser-known Sable Island horses are found in the east. Wild horse numbers have varied greatly over the years, but efforts are underway in all areas to protect and preserve these living legends.

COLORED
BREEDS

A beautiful overo Pinto stops at a pond for a late afternoon drink. Despite the registration eligibility of a wide variety of breeds and backgrounds, Pinto horse foal registrations are considerably less than those of American Paint Horses. Less than 5,000 Pinto foals were registered in 2005.

While our previous chapters have focused on breeds that have been grouped together because of their similar physical characteristics, this chapter on colored breeds is slightly different. The breed standards for the breeds covered in this chapter typically focus on color as one of the major criteria for registration. Animals that do not meet the standard for their breed's color are not usually granted full registration, although some registries, such as the American Paint Horse, offer a breeding stock section of their registry for horses that do not meet the color criteria for registration but still meet the breed's standard in other areas. For those horse enthusiasts who like something a little more unusual than the basic bay, black, or chestnut horse, let's explore the different types of colored horses.

The American Paint Horse is easily the most popular of the colored breeds and is one of the most popular breeds in the United States. Their unique and eye-catching coloring accentuates their other admirable qualities, such as their pleasant and trainable personalities. American Paint Horses are stock-type horses and are reminiscent of American Quarter Horses in type. Like the Quarter Horse, American Paint Horses are extremely popular choices for Western disciplines. The American Paint Horse Association recognizes several color variations, including tobiano, sabino, overo, tovero, and splash.

The American Paint Horse is one of the most popular breeds in America, with over 40,000 foals registered in 2005. Its kind temperament and stock-type build, not to mention its bonus of color, make it a popular choice with horse enthusiasts.

Unlike the American Paint Horse Association, which has restrictions on allowable breeds, the Pinto Horse Association of America will register horses of many breeds as long as they exhibit the necessary coloring. Pinto horses are recognized in tobiano and overo patterns. The popularity of the colored breeds remains very high in the United States.

The development of the distinctive and attractive Appaloosa is credited to the Nez Perce Indians. The name of the Appaloosa breed comes from the Palouse River in the northwestern United States. Today the Appaloosa is a very popular stock-type breed and is recognized in many color varieties, including blanket, frost, marble, snowflake, and leopard. The Appaloosa is one of the foundation breeds for the highly popular Pony of the Americas.

Because palomino coloring does not breed true and therefore cannot reproduce itself with regularity, it is not technically considered a breed. Having said that, however, it must be noted that the Palomino Horse Association in the United States issues registration papers to palomino horses that meet the registry's criteria of size, breed, and coloring. Palominos are prized for their golden coloring and are accompanied by a white mane and tail.

As with the Palomino, the Buckskin is also considered a color rather than a true breed. The International Buckskin Horse Association registers Buckskins of many different breeds. In addition, the registry recognizes several related colors, including duns and grullas. Buckskins have long been associated with hardiness and durability. There is an old saying, "You can't kill a Buckskin, he'll last and he'll last." This attractive golden breed is accentuated by a black mane, tail, and points, which makes it a very distinctive and desirable color.

Unlike the leopard pattern, which has dark spots over the horse's entire body, the spotted blanket Appaloosa pattern shown here has only a white blanket dotted with dark spots over the horse's hindquarters.

Combining the highly desirable characteristics of the Arabian with the striking coloring of the Pinto, the Pintabian horse's name is a combination of its foundation breed's names. Unlike the Pinto Horse Association of America, the Pintabian Horse Registry only recognizes the tobiano pattern of markings. Pintabians that do not exhibit tobiano markings cannot be registered in the Pintabian colored division, but may be registered in the breeding stock division or the Arabian outcross division. Pintabians consist of more than 99 percent but less than 100 percent Arabian blood.

The Knabstrup (or Knabstruper) is considerably more unusual than the similarly marked Appaloosa. While the Appaloosa breed was developed in North America, the Knabstrup was developed in Europe. Despite their different locales, both breeds are believed to descend from Spanish horses. The Knabstrup is found with many of the same color patterns as the Appaloosa and is very rare in the United States at this time.

The Pinto Horse Association of America (PtHA) recognizes the tobiano and overo color patterns and the registry is open to horses and ponies of many breeds, including Miniature Horses. The PtHA does, however, restrict registration from Appaloosas, mules, and draft horses.

This pale Palomino horse is a somewhat lighter shade than the ideal color of a "newly minted gold coin." Palominos that are especially light are sometimes called Isabella Palominos.

Always a popular and sought-after color, the Palomino is highly prized for its rich golden coat and accompanying white mane and tail. Palomino coloring is found in many horse and pony breeds. Any breed is eligible for registration with the Palomino Horse Association (PHA) as long as it exhibits the necessary palomino coloring. The PHA also recognizes cremello horses as Palomino breeding stock.

At first glance you might think that this horse would be considered a roan, but in actuality this is an Appaloosa pattern called a snowcap. If you look closely at this Appaloosa's face, you will see extensive face mottling.

Opposite: Characterized by its creamy golden coat and striking black points (mane, tail, and legs), the Buckskin is a perennial favorite among color enthusiasts. Many Buckskin horses are of American Quarter Horse ancestry, such as the one pictured here, although the International Buckskin Horse Registry does accept horses of other breeds as long as they meet the necessary color criteria.

Despite its stock-type American Quarter Horse breeding, this Buckskin has shown an affinity for English disciplines, particularly jumping, which aptly illustrates the Quarter Horse's versatility.

This Buckskin foal exhibits the unique eye coloring that is often found in buckskin and palomino horses. These amber-colored eyes almost appear transparent in certain lighting. This foal was born with deep blue eyes but they have lightened to the amber shade.

Elegant and beautiful, this Pintabian reflects the characteristics that the breed is known for: a lovely Arabian-type head with a dished profile that tapers to a tiny muzzle and the tobiano coloring that is found in Pinto horses.

One of the most striking of the Appaloosa color patterns, this stallion exhibits the leopard color pattern, which consists of a white base with dark spots that extends over the entire body without concentration to one particular area.

Palomino horses are especially striking when they have white markings to accentuate their white manes and tails. This colt exhibits a minimal splash white color pattern in addition to his palomino color.

Although Appaloosas are well-known for their suitability for Western disciplines, the breed is very versatile and many participate in other disciplines. This solid blanket Appaloosa is pulling a cart.

Opposite: Its calm and docile temperament makes the American Paint Horse a wonderful choice for an all-around family horse.

Like the American Quarter Horse, the American Paint Horse is often found participating in Western disciplines, such as the Western pleasure class seen here.

Left: Appaloosas are found in a variety of color patterns, but they also share common characteristics, including easily visible white sclera of the eye and mottled skin, both of which are apparent on the face of this Appaloosa horse. Appaloosas also typically have striped hooves.

Opposite: Pinto and palomino are two interesting colors that have combined in the horse shown here. This attractively colored horse is enjoying a quiet morning grazing in his meadow.

Strikingly beautiful, this American Paint Horse exhibits frame overo markings, which are distinguishable because the white does not extend over the horse's back and also because of the white marking present on the horse's face. Accented against the deep black of the horse's base color, this is an impressive and eye-catching color combination.

This halter class at an American Paint Horse show illustrates the wide variety in the amount of white markings that can be found on Paint Horses. In fact, it is common for American Paint Horse foals to be born without the desired white markings. These foals are designated as "breeding stock" American Paint Horses.

Regardless of their color, the colored breeds, such as Appaloosa, American Paint Horse, Pinto, Buckskin, and Palomino, find their greatest attributes in their abilities, talent, and temperament. These factors make them useful breeds for many activities.

Opposite: A unique combination of two Appaloosa color patterns are found here on one horse. This Appaloosa exhibits the spotted blanket pattern as well as the snowflake pattern, which is responsible for the fleckings of white roaning along the horse's neck, chest, and head.

The sabino color pattern frequently seen in American Paint Horses is said to be a type of overo. The sabino pattern (*sabino* means "speckled" in Spanish) is characterized by white markings that have jagged or roaned edges, as well as a white spot on the lower lip or chin, as depicted on this horse.

The Appaloosa's distinctive coloring combines with other positive qualities, such as good temperament, stamina, and natural athletic talent, to make the breed a long-time favorite of horse owners.

Opposite: Another type of Appaloosa coloring that is similar in looks to the snowcap pattern is the varnish pattern. Note the darker colored portions of the horse's body, such as the legs, ears, and shoulders. These are the typical characteristics of the varnish pattern.

Grazing in this picturesque meadow are two colored horses: a striking black-and-white overo Pinto and a gorgeous golden Palomino. Color enthusiasts strive for horses with the same qualities of conformation and breed type that other horse owners seek—they just like to find them in more colorful packaging! This scene is a color enthusiast's dream come true.

HEAVY HORSES

Although many Gypsy Vanners feature black and white coloring, they can be found in any color or color pattern. All colors are eligible for registration within the Gypsy Vanner Horse Society.

Now that we have discussed the diminutive pony breeds, the multitude of light horse breeds, and the eye-catching color breeds, it's time to turn our attention to the largest equines: the heavy draft breeds. These substantial breeds have been utilized for centuries as work horses on farms and in forests, as war horses, and as providers of transportation.

Heavy horse breeds are built differently than their lighter horse counterparts. They are substantial creatures with massive muscling and size, matched by impressive height and width. These breeds typically range from 16 to 17 hands in height, although some individuals (particularly in breeds such as the Shire or the Belgian) can reach heights in excess of 18 hands. These breeds have heavy bones, large hooves, deep heart girths, and compact builds. Their heads often feature a convex profile or Roman nose.

Heavy draft horses are sometimes called "gentle giants" because they are renowned for having excellent temperaments, are quiet and sensible, and are not flighty at all. While they do possess incredible power, strength, and stamina, their size and weight often disguise their true dispositions. They are often honest and hardworking with cooperative natures and are willing to please their owners. To the farmer working in the fields or the logger working in the forests, these draft horses were (and are still today) often like family members. The horses are

The Percheron is said to have been considerably influenced by the Arabian breed, as seen in this team of Percherons. Their grey coloring as well as the added refinement in their faces are a result of the Arabian heritage.

trustworthy and willing, and they work side by side, day after day, to complete their necessary tasks.

As the presence of tractors and other farm equipment has increased over time, the necessity of these work horses on farms has decreased, and subsequently the population of these breeds has also decreased. Today, several heavy horse breeds are listed on the American Livestock Breeds Conservancy's Conservation Priority List. Currently listed as critical (global population of less than 2,000)

The Gypsy Vanner is a smaller draft horse that usually exhibits pinto coloration and is quickly gaining a great deal of attention with horse owners in the United States. This herd of Gypsies enjoys a romp in the pasture when their owner calls "Grain time!"

are the American Cream Draft and the Suffolk Punch. The Clydesdale and the Shire are on the watch list (global population of less than 10,000). Currently listed as recovering are the Belgian and the Percheron, although they are still being closely monitored, and the Irish Draught is currently under study. Devoted enthusiasts continue to raise and promote these breeds for the future to ensure their presence for years to come.

While not as commonly seen as some of the other draft breeds, the North American Spotted Draft Horse is beginning to be noticed by fans of draft horses who are intrigued by the breed's distinctive coat coloring. This horse is taking a rest after an English pleasure class at an open horse show, which demonstrates the breed's usefulness as a riding mount.

Let's take a look at some of the breeds that make up the heavy draft horse type. The Belgian Draft originated, as its name implies, in Belgium. The breed is said to have descended from the Medieval Great Horse and is also known as the Brabant in Europe. The first Belgians were imported to the United States in the late 1800s to be used on Midwestern farms. Belgian enthusiasts in the United States call their breed "America's favorite draft horse," due to the fact that there are more Belgians in the United States than all other draft breeds combined. Nowadays the Belgian is popular as a harness horse and is used in weight-pulling competitions and also for driving. They are massive horses and noted for their strength and durability.

While not as populous as the Belgian, the Clydesdale is probably more easily recognized by Americans, thanks to the well-known Budweiser advertising campaign featuring impressive eight-horse hitches of Clydesdale horses. Unlike the Belgian, which is universally chestnut with white markings, Clydesdales are usually a darker color, such as bay or black, with white stockings and extensive sabino markings and roaning. The Clydesdale originated in Scotland from an area called Clyde, and the foundation breeds included Belgian and Shire horses, as well as native draft horses. The Clydesdale is noted for having a more attractive head than some of the other draft breeds, and it is also somewhat smaller and more refined than other draft horses.

Power, elegance, and strength. This dappled grey Percheron is shown in a draft harness hitched to a handsome two-wheeled Meadowbrook cart. It is a truly picturesque scene.

Another breed that is popular with draft hitches is the Percheron, a breed that is comprised of mainly greys, although the occasional black is also seen. Their predominantly grey coloring is attributed to many infusions of Arabian blood into the breed during the eighteenth and nineteenth centuries. Arabian characteristics are also seen in the Percheron's head. Its movement is also influenced by its Arabian heritage, as the Percheron exhibits a longer stride than many of the other draft breeds. Percherons have historically been used for farm work, as war horses, and as driving animals. The Percheron originated in France and is named for the Le Perche region. There are currently more Percherons in the United States than in any other country, including France.

As the name implies, the Shire is a British breed noted for its excellent pulling ability and docile temperament. This massive breed is also noted for its heavily feathered legs, long neck, and incredible bone and substance. Like the Clydesdale, the Shire often possesses white leg markings and a blaze, although the sabino roaning is not usually seen on the Shire. (It is actually viewed as undesirable, according to the American Shire Horse Association breed standard.) The most common Shire colors are bay, black, brown, and grey.

Another smaller British breed is the Suffolk Punch Heavy Horse, usually known as the Suffolk or Suffolk Punch. All of today's Suffolks descend from one stallion, Thomas Crisp's Horse of Ufford, from the eighteenth century. The Suffolk Punch is shorter-legged than some of the other draft breeds and has much less feathering than the Shire or Clydesdale, which makes it a valuable asset to farmers who use horses to work in heavy clay soil. Suffolks are noted for their longevity and are always a shade of chestnut (known as *chesnut* without the "t" in the Suffolk breed).

This black Percheron demonstrates the breed's pulling ability at a winter festival in front of an enthusiastic audience. These events are quite popular throughout the United States. While most Percherons (including the one pictured) range in size between 16 and 17.2 hands, some have grown to be over 20 hands.

Two heavy draft breeds have been developed on American soil, both of which are colored varieties of the traditional heavy draft breeds: the North American Spotted Draft Horse and the American Cream Draft. The North American Spotted Draft is a multi-colored version of the typical heavy horse and exhibits characteristics of a Belgian, Percheron, or Shire, but with the addition of pinto coat coloring.

Strength, style, stamina, and a dash of charisma are all wrapped up in a massive equine package. This Belgian is participating in a draft pulling competition where it is displaying the qualities and characteristics that make the breed so popular. The Belgian is said to be America's favorite draft horse.

The North American Spotted Draft Horse Association (NASDHA) was established in 1995 and has since registered more than 3,000 Spotted Drafts. The American Cream Draft Registry is considerably older than the NASDHA and was established in 1944. Unlike the Suffolk Punch, which is easily traced to a specific foundation sire, the American Cream Draft traces back to an instrumental foundation dam, Old Granny, who produced several cream-colored draft foals at the beginning of the twentieth century.

It took the luck o' the Irish to produce the Irish Draught, a draft breed that features a bit more refinement than is found is some of the other draft breeds. Some sources say that this refinement is due to infusions of Andalusian and Connemara blood. While many draft breeds are primarily used for driving or pulling, the Irish Draught is also a quality riding horse. It is a lighter type of draft horse that still possesses draft qualities, yet offers a versatility that is prized by enthusiasts.

Another breed with Irish heritage is the Gypsy Vanner, a smaller draft horse that is rapidly gaining popularity in the United States. Although the American registry for Gypsy Vanner horses was only recently established (1996), these horses have been bred as caravan horses in Great Britain for decades. They are noted for their strength, friendly dispositions, trainability, and striking appearance. All colors and markings are acceptable, although many Gypsy Vanner horses are pinto. The Gypsy Vanner's heritage includes influence from larger breeds, such as the Clydesdale, Friesian, and Shire, as well as influence from native pony breeds, like the Dales Pony.

A pair of Belgian Draft Horses are pulling a heavy load. Note the way the team is working together to pull into their harness as a unit in order to pull the load behind them.

"Pulling Horses!" An enthusiastic draft horse exhibitor's horse trailer proudly displays this sign, which announces its participation in draft horse pulling events.

Opposite: Draft horses in competition or regular work must be specially shod and wear unique shoes, as seen here. The design of the shoes helps prevent the horses from slipping, which is especially important when they work during the winter on icy or snow-covered terrain.

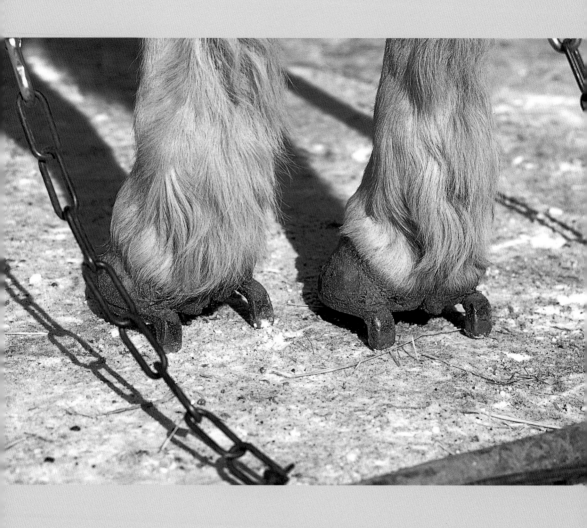

Many Percherons, such as this one, are grey and are still noticeably influenced by the breed's early infusions of Arabian blood. This Percheron was foaled black and is slowly turning grey as she matures. In a few more years, there will probably be no black coloring left on her at all.

Opposite: Although Clydesdales originated in Scotland, today more are found in the United States than in any other country. Yet they are still on the American Livestock Breed Conservancy's watch list.

A unicorn hitch of Percheron horses with a black leader and a grey team behind is shown here. The black horse in front is considerably larger than the grey horses, which is an ideal attribute for the leader of a hitch.

A sleigh ride is always a popular attraction at any event. This sleigh is being pulled by a matched team of Belgians and is a picture-perfect moment on a snowy winter day for this lucky group of people.

This team of grey Percherons is pulling a large sleigh at a winter festival in northern Wisconsin. There are few sights as impressive as that of a draft team and a sleigh full of people enjoying a pleasant winter afternoon.

A pair of black Percheron mares enjoy a quiet day at pasture. Although they are aged mares, they still happily perform their duties of pulling a sleigh in the winter months.

All dressed up and off to a show. This black Percheron's tail has been adorned with ribbons and bows, which is traditional turnout for an in-hand class for Percherons. While the added frills do not influence the judge's decision, they do signify that the exhibitor has taken the time and effort to pay attention to detail.

Opposite: The harness worn by these black Percherons is very impressive, but so is the fantastic show wagon pulled behind them.

These Shires are grazing peacefully
in a lush pasture reminiscent of their
native land, the United Kingdom.
The Shire Horse Society was formed
in 1884 and the breed received its
name from this organization.

Unlike many of the other heavy draft breeds that have been decreasing in numbers, it is said that the Shire is increasing in popularity. The Shire's foundation breeds included the Friesian and the Flanders horse.

Opposite: The breed standard for the Gypsy Vanner Horse Society states that Gypsy Vanners should possess abundant feathering on the legs. The Gypsy Vanner seen here certainly meets that criteria.

After a lifetime of hard work on the farm, this aged pair of Belgian geldings are now enjoying the well-earned days of their retirement. Days of effort and cooperation are replaced by days of grazing, napping, and relaxing under a blanket of autumn color.

A yearling Percheron gelding poses
for the judge during a halter class at
a county fair. Although he is too young
to be shown in driving classes, he is
gaining experience and education by
being groomed, trailered, and shown,
which are all valuable lessons for a
young horse to learn.

Looking resplendent in their show harness, this beautiful team of Belgian mares complete their performance at a county fair. Devoted draft driving enthusiasts prize the Belgian.

Masses of bone coupled with strong and powerful hindquarters make it easy to see why these Belgians are such a popular choice for draft hitches and pulling contests. Their immense strength and power might be overwhelming for a horse owner if it weren't for the Belgian's quiet and tractable disposition.

A calm and pleasant disposition is another of the Gypsy Vanner's attributes.
These foals are grooming each other, which is a popular pastime with youngsters.

This is a perfectly matched unicorn hitch (one horse in front, a pair of horses behind) of Clydesdale horses preparing for a demonstration at a state fair. They are a remarkable sight in their shining show harnesses with coats groomed to perfection.

Draft horse shows remain very popular at county fairs nationwide. This sign was photographed on a barn at a county fair in the Upper Peninsula of Michigan, where draft horses have a large following and receive a great deal of enthusiasm from exhibitors and spectators alike.

Opposite: Time for a rest. This team of Belgians is enjoying a quiet moment of relaxation before their next event.

Today, the Shire is often found with bay coloring, as shown here. However, the breed's coloring was originally black and the Shire was originally called the "English Black." The subsequent rise of other colors, such as bay, brown, and grey, made the name change necessary.

Some heavy horse breeds, such as the Shire or the Clydesdale (shown here), possess extensive white markings: high white stockings, blazes, and even belly spots. Other heavy horse breeds, such as the Percheron, display considerably less markings.

The qualities of a draft horse are not strictly limited to purebred animals. Draft horses often make excellent crosses with other breeds, such as the Shire-Thoroughbred horse seen here. The athleticism of the Thoroughbred, combined with the quiet temperament and strength of the draft horse, make an excellent combination.

A large Shire draft horse is dozing in the sunshine next to her Chincoteague Pony companion. Size does not seem to matter when horses become friends. When a pony is pastured with a horse, it's often the pony that ends up in charge of things, such as who eats first.

As opposed to the impressive beauty of a draft horse's show harness, the working harness for pulling is all about practicality and usefulness. These Belgians are busily working on a summer afternoon.

Opposite: Although many Gypsy Vanners feature black and white coloring, they can be found in any color or color pattern. All colors are eligible for registration within the Gypsy Vanner Horse Society.

Although chestnut is the most common and desired color of Belgians in America, other colors are also found. Because chestnut coloring breeds true (chestnut crossed with chestnut equals chestnut, every time), it's easy for Belgian enthusiasts to specifically select their desired color.

Many draft horse breeds possess extensive white markings on their legs and faces, such as the Belgians seen here. Their wide blazes extend all the way down over their muzzles and are characteristic of the sabino pattern of white markings that is often found on heavy horse breeds such as the Clydesdale and Shire.

Muscling and ample substance are two
of the most important characteristics of
the heavy draft breeds. This Percheron
fully exhibits these traits.

An incredible amount of preparation is necessary before a draft horse show. The harness, both leather and silver portions, must be thoroughly cleaned and polished to finish the overall presentation.

Heavy horses have been used in farm work and in forests for logging for centuries. This team of Belgians is pulling a heavy load of logs during a demonstration to illustrate the hard work that these horses do so well.

This Percheron is ready for her in-hand class at a show and is fully prepared with a white show bridle and a plaited mane with accent bows. These impressive animals are well turned out for their halter classes. The added adornment of the fancy show attire makes the entire picture complete.

5

DONKEYS AND MULES

The draft mule, easily identified by its distinctive length of ear, is an intelligent creature that combines the characteristics of the draft horse with those of the mule. It is popular as a trail mount, although some owners enjoy showing their mules.

I n a league of their own are the long-eared equines: the distinctive donkey and the equally memorable mule. No discussion of horses would be complete without a mention of these special creatures.

Different from their horse cousins in many respects, donkeys and mules are obviously notable because of their exceptionally long ears, but also because of their somewhat plain heads, sparseness of mane and tail, and their overall conformation. Donkeys come in many sizes, from the miniature Mediterranean donkey that stands less than 36 inches to the Standard and Large Standard donkeys that stand between 36 and 56 inches, all the way up to the Mammoth Stock donkeys, which are larger than 54 inches.

Donkeys are noted for their unique coloring and their distinctive braying sound. They have long been utilized as pack animals and are sometimes used as livestock guardians to protect smaller farm animals, such as sheep, from predators.

A mule is the offspring of a male donkey and a female horse. The resulting mule exhibits characteristics of the donkey and the horse. In the case of a cross between a horse stallion and a female donkey, the resulting offspring is known as a hinny rather than a mule. In either case, hinnies and mules are sterile and unable to produce offspring. Therefore, any mule or hinny is the product of a cross between a horse and a donkey.

A matched pair of draft mules in harness are shown here. This pair is a full brother and sister, which means that they have the same sire and dam. In this case it is a donkey sire and a draft horse dam. Because of their donkey/horse background, mules typically exhibit more horse-like characteristics than donkeys.

As is the case with donkeys, mules come in a wide variety of sizes, from the diminutive miniature mule all the way up to large draft mules, which are produced by crossing a draft horse mare with a Mammoth jack donkey. Draft mules are popular pack animals and have historical importance as they were often used during the westward expansion of the United States. The expression "stubborn as a mule" may give some insight into the personalities of these animals, but enthusiasts maintain that the mule's qualities and good characteristics far outweigh any stubbornness in their nature.

Although donkeys typically require less concentrated feed than horses, they still need access to good-quality hay and pasture to maintain good health. This donkey is happily grazing and enjoying a tasty meal.

Previous spread, left: This mule exhibits black coloring accompanied by ears with lighter tips and lighter rims around his eyes. He also exhibits the lighter-colored muzzle that is often seen on mules and donkeys.

Previous spread, right: In proportion to its body, a donkey's ears are considerably longer than a horse's. This photo clearly illustrates the impressive length of a donkey's ears, which are all a part of the donkey's charm.

Opposite: Like draft horses, draft mules are useful for draft harness work. These draft mules have just completed a presentation of draft hitches in a parade at a county fair.

A mule pulls an elegant wagon in New Orleans, Louisiana. Mules are versatile creatures and excel in many different areas.

Here is a close-up of the shoulder cross for which donkeys are noted. Donkeys often exhibit other types of primitive markings, including dorsal stripes and leg barring.

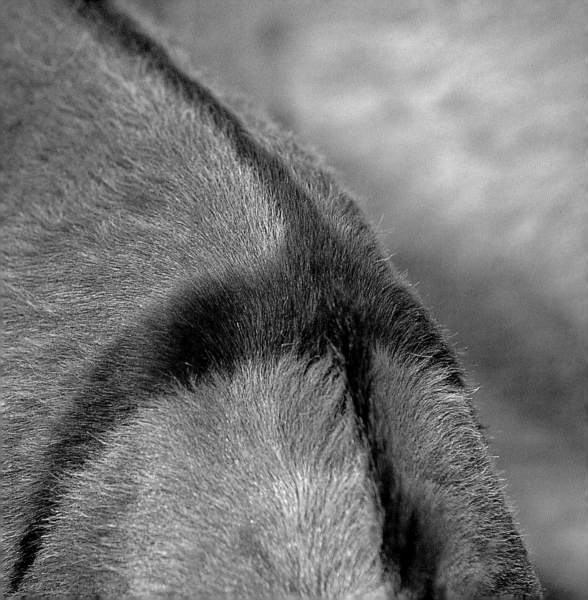

Donkeys are found in many colors, from black to cream to roan, but this donkey is an example of the traditional grey coloring that most people think of when they picture a donkey. Note the leg barring and the shoulder cross that this donkey exhibits.

INDEX